Becoming a Master Communicator

PRAISE FOR *BECOMING A MASTER COMMUNICATOR* AND RENÉE MARINO

"When it comes to helping you authentically communicate, Renée Marino is the woman to do that!"

— Clint Eastwood, Actor, Producer, and Director

"Most people don't consider themselves good communicators. However, it's a fact that deliberate, confident, and results-driven communication is the cornerstone to a successful business, meaningful relationships, and an abundant life. Renée has made it her obsession to help everyday people master communication with simple processes and tools. If you strive for higher purpose or success, then learning these principles is a must."

— Dean Graziosi, Multiple *New York Times* Best-Selling Author, Entrepreneur, and Top Business Strategist

"Renée was the dance captain on the Broadway musical I was working on back in 2017. No, I wasn't dancing—I was the songwriter—but watching her take on the music and invigorate and inspire the entire cast was a treat. I'm sure you'll find these same attributes in her book…and without a step out of place."

— Bryan Adams, Songwriter

"Technology is ever-changing. Human connection is not. This book is a beautiful guide in bridging the gap between technology and human connection when it comes to our communication skills."

— Dhomonique Murphy, 3x Emmy Award Winning Journalist, Founder of Mediamasterynow.com and TheRightMethod.com

"There is nothing more powerful than being able to make a complicated topic simple and easy to understand. Renée Marino has made one of the most difficult parts of our life—communication—simple. Her tools and strategies are packed with value in helping us make stronger connections in our businesses and in our individual relationships."

— Russell Brunson, Co-Founder of ClickFunnels

"The internet has taken away our ability to feel for each other, to touch, to be human again. All the credentials in the world mean nothing if you can't communicate. Renée Marino has brilliantly merged the two worlds of the internet and human contact and how they can help you on the road to success. Her book should be required reading for anyone with a dream."

— Chazz Palminteri, Actor, Writer, and Director

"If you've ever struggled with communication or dreamt of being a confident communicator, this is the book for you. Through Renée's powerful stories to the tactical information that you can apply today, this book walks you through mastering communication and infusing your gifts into the way you show up in the world, allowing you to make a bigger impact. From honing in on your go-to style of communication to understanding the role technology plays in the way we show up, this book will guide you through the information in an entertaining and enlightening way."

— Jenna Kutcher, Host of The Goal Digger Podcast

"Renée Marino has cracked the code on one of the biggest challenges facing us today—tech versus touch. With humor and with candor, she illustrates how easy it is to sacrifice our relationships with ourselves and with others, as traditional communication skills are sacrificed by modern conveniences. Her simple (but effective) strategies for living intentionally offer practical choices to restore balance, lean into authenticity, and live a life fully expressed."

— Bari Baumgardner, Founder of SAGE Event Management

"*Becoming a Master Communicator* is the answer to a question our world is asking right now: How do we use digital technology to keep us connected in our business and personal lives without diminishing our humanity? Through these pages, Renée Marino clearly and lovingly shows us the way!"

—Stuart K Robinson, Entertainment CEO, Motivational Speaker, Author

"If you are looking for simple and easy-to-implement practices to improve your communication, *this* is the book for you. Renée Marino is the master at delivering strategies you can implement immediately to improve both your business and personal relationships. Thank you, Renée!"

— Pat Quinn, Founder of Storylinq.com

"Renée is someone who lights up every room she walks into with her infectious energy. She motivates and inspires people everywhere she goes with her positivity and zest for life. I've always thought if you could bottle her energy and passion, everyone would be lining up to get it, and now you can in this book. I am so excited for you to be inspired by this wonderful woman!"

— Samantha Barks, Star of Stage and Screen

"In *Becoming a Master Communicator*, Renée Marino shows us not only how to communicate well, but when to use or not use technology for communication, and how to learn to speak up for ourselves without fearing confrontation. Filled with personal stories and examples, including how she landed the lead female role in the film *Jersey Boys*, this book is chock-full of humor, insight, and ultimately personal freedom from the things keeping you from living your best life. Don't miss this rare treat that you will want to revisit again and again as you become a master communicator."

— Tyler R. Tichelaar, PhD and Award-Winning Author of
Narrow Lives and *When Teddy Came to Town*

"Words matter! Using our ability to communicate, to find common ground with anyone, anytime, anywhere is the key to a successful life and business. Renée's book holds the answer to this incredible skill. I can't imagine a more powerful tool to take our communication, our leadership, and our influence to the next level!"

— Otilia Kiss, Results Coach and Business Trainer

"Renée Marino is the queen of breakthrough communication! Her techniques are exactly what is needed to create balance with technology…to use it for good, while empowering your personal and work relationships. Be prepared for the entertaining stories in this book that will serve as a mirror and motivation toward creating authentic connections where they count in your daily life."

— Christine Gail, Best-Selling Author of *Unleash Your Rising*, Story Breakthrough Leadership Strategist, and Book Publishing Coach

"How we communicate with others is crucial to the quality of our lives. Most of us have become too reliant on texts and emails rather than the good old-fashioned way of picking up the phone or speaking to someone face-to-face. Renée Marino is on a mission to create awareness of the importance of the way we communicate with each other and provides us with practical lessons on how to effectively do just that. She merges today's technology with 'Ol' School Simplicity' and shares practical lessons on getting your message across to others in a clear and direct way. This book will inspire you to show up as your most authentic self, encourage you to express your truth fearlessly, and prod you to let go of perfection by taking 'imperfect action.' It's a book about communication, but it is also packed with life lessons to empower and enrich your life!"

— Gloria Carpenter, Professional Singer and Author of *Power Up Your Dreams! Moving From Self-Defeat to Self-Belief*

"Renée has a great understanding of how communication works, and she can show you how to use communication to improve your life and achieve your goals instead of letting poor communication disrupt them."

— Stephen Murray, Business Consultant

"I loved this book because it is Renée's authentic self speaking to you and me! Renée's passion for helping people see the importance in making that human connection in our communications is on every page. Drawing on her own personal experiences, including her professional life as an actress, she uses it all to relate to our struggles around communication with today's technology as only she can. I am so grateful for how she challenges and encourages people to step up their communication, to get back to connecting with one another, and gives permission to take imperfect action to do it!"

— Jason Blount, Breakthrough Coach

"*Becoming a Master Communicator* will show you how to improve the way you connect, be more authentic, have more influence, stay open, be concise, and be clear! If you are like me and want to get back to reclaiming and rebuilding your confidence, have more fulfilling relationships, and create more success and effectiveness in your career, this is the right book at the right time! Renée helps you become a master communicator in ways that are not only inspiring, fun, and to the point, but fully engaging too. In such a short time with Renée as my coach, I was able to transform my confidence, skills, and effectiveness as a master communicator by taking constant imperfect action. This book arms you with everything you need to learn to use technology without being overdependent on it. You will improve and become a better communicator!"

— Lorraine Thomson, Author and Life and Entrepreneur Coach

"Don't hesitate; buy the book! Everyone can benefit from this book! It gives a straight-to-the-point explanation and examples of how technology has caused pain points in our human interactions and communication, but more importantly, Renée showcases the positives and the gifts that technology provides, and solutions for how to mitigate the gaps and issues technology is causing. The Reflections Sections are great and really allow us to take accountability and responsibility in making a positive change and creating positive impact. It is an easy and fun read that makes you feel like you are sitting on the couch talking with Renée. This is a book I would highly recommend!"

— Jana Swenson, International Speaker, Mindset Coach, and Breakthrough Expert

BECOMING A MASTER COMMUNICATOR

Balancing New School Technology with Ol' School Simplicity

RENÉE MARINO

NEW YORK

LONDON • NASHVILLE • MELBOURNE • VANCOUVER

Becoming a Master Communicator

Balancing New School Technology with Ol' School Simplicity

Published in New York, New York, by Morgan James Publishing. Morgan James is a trademark of Morgan James, LLC. www.MorganJamesPublishing.com

Proudly distributed by Ingram Publisher Services.

Some of the names in the book have been changed to protect individual's privacy. Every attempt has been made to source all quotes properly.

For additional copies or bulk purchases visit:
ReneeMarino.com

Morgan James BOGO™

A **FREE** ebook edition is available for you or a friend with the purchase of this print book.

CLEARLY SIGN YOUR NAME ABOVE

Instructions to claim your free ebook edition:
1. Visit MorganJamesBOGO.com
2. Sign your name CLEARLY in the space above
3. Complete the form and submit a photo of this entire page
4. You or your friend can download the ebook to your preferred device

ISBN 9781631956003 paperback
ISBN 9781631956041 ebook
Library of Congress Control Number:
2021936677

Cover Design by:
Rachel Lopez
www.r2cdesign.com

Interior Design by:
Christopher Kirk
www.GFSstudio.com

Editors:
Tyler Tichelaar and Larry Alexander,
Superior Book Productions

Author Photo:
Daryl A. Getman

Morgan James is a proud partner of Habitat for Humanity Peninsula and Greater Williamsburg. Partners in building since 2006.

Get involved today! Visit MorganJamesPublishing.com/giving-back

For my Father Frank in Heaven. Your ability to clearly and consistently communicate your love, guidance, and support is what planted the seed for this book to be able to grow. Thank you for being a Master Communicator.

I am blessed to be your daughter.

ACKNOWLEDGMENTS

There are so very many people I need to thank and honor, for their support in bringing this book into existence. Thank you, God, for the gift of this life, and choosing me to have this book be written through.

To the one by my side every single step of the journey—my selfless husband and best friend, Michael. Thank you from the deepest part of my soul for your unconditional love and support. You are my greatest teacher and inspiration, and I am so blessed to have you as my partner in this life. Thank you for cooking dinner, cleaning the house, and taking care of everything while I took the time to write this book. I love you with everything I am. Thank you to my beautiful mother for reminding me of my strengths when I sometimes forget them. I'm so proud to be your daughter, and I love you with my heart and soul. Thank you, big shit, for being the most incredible father, and now my angel watching over me as I write and always. I love you entirely and miss you wholly. Thank you to my entire family, and chosen family, for being the absolute best support system a person could hope for. You have helped to shape me into the woman I am and I love you all deeply. To my book coach, Christine Gail, thank you for your amazing guidance throughout this process, and thank you to David Hancock and Morgan James Publishing for making me a part of the family.

Thank you to my editors Tyler Tichelaar and Larry Alexander for giving me another perspective.

Thank you to the cast and crew of *Pretty Woman: The Musical* for your inspiration during the beginnings of this book. Special thanks to Hailei Call for being my very first editor, Billy Wright Sr. and Billy Wright Jr. for letting me use your offices between numbers so I could write, and Tommy Bracco for lending me your beach house so I could have my own writer's retreat.

Thank you, Jessica Meier, for always going the extra mile to turn my hopes into a reality.

Thank you to every person who took the time to be another set of eyes for me by reading a chapter or many, and providing feedback. Claire Gutbrod, Chelsea Wright, Nicole Jurick, Christopher Semidey-Zarate, Jana Swenson, Jennifer Rodriguez, Otilia Kiss, Rachel Burcham, Lorraine Thomson, Gloria Carpenter, Jason Blount, Stephen Murray, and Shawn Andersyn-your help was immeasurable.

To every single person mentioned in this book, thank you for being a part of my story.

To Clint Eastwood, Dean Graziosi, Bryan Adams, Russell Brunson, Chazz Palminteri, Dhomonique Murphy, Stuart K. Robinson, Jenna Kutcher, Bari Baumgardner, Pat Quinn, and Samantha Barks, I am honored you endorsed this book. Thank you from the bottom of my heart.

Thank you, Tony Robbins and Dean Graziosi, for being monumental in kicking off my path to becoming a communication coach.

To my clients, thank you for choosing me to be your coach. Your breakthroughs are my breakthroughs.

Thank you to each and every loving soul throughout my life in the form of a mentor, teacher, or friend, who has had faith in me, stood by me, and encouraged me to keep going in the pursuit of my dreams. You've left a profound imprint on my heart.

Finally, thank you, my reader, for whom this book was created. Your willingness to go on this journey of becoming a master communicator with an open heart and open mind fills me with complete gratitude. You mean the world to me, and I cannot wait to see where this book takes you!

CONTENTS

INTRODUCTION

"Communication is power. Those who have mastered its effective use can change their own experience of the world, and the world's experience of them. All behavior and feelings find their original roots in some form of communication."
— Tony Robbins

We are in such a powerful time of existence when we have everything and anything at our fingertips because of what I like to term *"New School Technology."* With applications like Facetime, Zoom, Skype, and Marco Polo, we are able to see our loved ones, some of whom live thousands of miles away, as if they live next door. With the power we possess from these outlets comes a lot of responsibility. We can be, do, or have anything at lightning speed because of new school technology, and the steady progression of it is a huge leap for us as a species. What I am finding, though, is that like with most things in life, when such a huge gain happens in one area, something has to be lost in another. That something is authentic verbal communication. Have you ever found yourself in a situation where vital information or important feelings were miscommunicated or not communicated at all, and you ended up in a conflict with a colleague or loved one? Maybe it caused you to miss the boat on a great opportunity? Was this due to a lack of face-to-face interaction? Perhaps it involved an email or text message gone wrong, or was caused by a general over-reliance on technology?

I will bet the answer is yes, because with the extraordinary convenience of technology, we are being propelled to connect with each other more often through a screen than directly, and as a result, clear communication can often take a backseat.

With technology being in the fast lane of progress, if we do not better equip ourselves with tools that create balance in our ever-changing communication world, we are headed toward a deep disconnect in our relationships.

Before we continue, I have some questions for you. Please be completely honest with yourself in answering them because this is the start of our journey together and self-assessment is a big part of that journey. The more honest you are, the more you open the door to positive transformation. These questions may concern both your personal and business life, so here they are:

- Are you more comfortable communicating from behind the screen of your computer or your phone than in person?
- Does the thought of "speaking your mind" scare the heck out of you?
- Do you wish you had more overall confidence to take the next step in your relationship or career?

If you answered yes to one or more of these questions, then this book is going to become your new best friend. To celebrate you for taking this journey with me, I have created a special gift to set you up for success. Right now, go to FreeGiftFromRenee.com and download the "Master Communicators Soul Contract." This contract was created for you to honor yourself in taking the action to becoming a master communicator and hold yourself accountable throughout the journey. Print it out, and after you sign and date it, keep the contract in your line of vision every day as a reminder of why you started the journey!

Now that you've done that, I can't wait for you to dig in and allow me to share what I know so deeply in my soul to be true:

Communication is the foundation of all of our relationships.

As a professional communication coach, I have shared this idea time and time again when clients, friends, and coworkers have come to me asking for advice about how to improve their relationships. Their requests made me recognize a common need for guidance in this area, especially because of how technology has evolved the way we communicate. Cognitive neuroscientist Adam Gazzaley and psychologist Larry Rosen stated in *The Distracted Mind*:

> So many technological innovations have enhanced our lives in countless ways, but they also threaten to overwhelm our brain's goal-directed functioning with interference.... It impacts every level of our thinking, from our perceptions, decision making, communication, emotional regulation and our memories.[1]

Through observing myself and others as we move about in this culture, I have realized a common trend that is causing obstacles for many of us in our personal and professional relationships:

We have allowed technology to become our crutch for communication.

While living in this digitally-saturated culture, I have seen firsthand the communication challenges my clients face, including a lack of confidence in communicating beyond the screens of their devices, how to speak up when they want to share ideas at work or in their significant relationships, and how to translate the openness they have on social media to in-person

---

1   Gazzaley, Adam and Larry D. Rosen. *The Distracted Mind: Ancient Brains in a High-Tech World.* Cambridge, MA: MIT Press, 2016.

conversations. These are in addition to my own experienced challenges, which I'll be sharing with you throughout this book. See, all of these challenges make total sense because we've become so accustomed to using our cellphones and computers for everything, as if they are extensions of our being, and that includes in our communication with one another.

I knew in my soul that this book needed to be written, so a light of awareness could shine on this trend. Once we are aware, we can take the accountability necessary to move beyond using our smartphones, iPads, and laptops as our only sources for connecting with one another.

The purpose of this book is to guide you in using technology as a tool, but not the only tool, in communicating with others!

That said, I believe technology is a *gift* to this world! Each and every day I pick up my smartphone or open my laptop to connect with a client or friend, I thank my lucky stars for the gift of technology. My intention for this book is not to downplay that gift, but rather to help us use technology in its most powerful form: *as an agent to improve communication within our relationships and not inhibit it.* Communication has been one of the greatest driving forces in my life, which is why I'm so passionate about helping you become a master of it. I was nurtured in a home where open communication with one another was a constant, and that communication was done through verbal conversations, and not screens of any kind.

In my previous career as an actress on Broadway, in film, television, and on tours for sixteen years, I acquired one of the most incredible opportunities of my life because I had the confidence to verbally communicate from my heart. (Don't worry; I'll give you all the details in a future chapter, but here are a few highlights!) I had the honor of playing the female lead role of *Mary Delgado* in the film *Jersey Boys*, directed by Clint Eastwood. Not only did I get the chance to tell an incredible story as an actor, but I was also mentored by the legend himself—Clint Eastwood. I had front row seats to viewing how in the workplace, transparent and honest communication from a leader trickles down to the rest of the team, making for a positive and productive atmosphere. This experience made me understand a fundamental lesson in business:

A leader, whether on a film set, in a corporate setting, or anywhere else must be a master communicator!

Now, you may be asking yourself, "What the heck is a 'Master Communicator,' exactly?" I'm so excited to answer that for you. A "Master Communicator" is a person who communicates clearly and effectively in their personal and professional relationships by knowing the right time to use their devices in their interactions, and the right time to put the devices down and simply have a real conversation.

I mean, how many times have you had a back-and-forth conversation with someone for hours but never spoken to them or physically seen them because your fingers made the conversation through text or email? Sure, this may be fine in some situations, but when you constantly communicate this way, you are losing what I call, *"Ol' School Simplicity."*

Ol' School Simplicity refers to the more intimate channels of communication used before computers became part of our everyday lives. These ways included in-person conversations, phone calls, and handwritten letters.

Now, you could be thinking handwritten letters are similar to email or text, but they are quite different. In handwritten letters, the thoughts and emotions of the person writing are reflected in the way they draw the words on the page—this is a personal touch that cannot be replicated by a computer.

With all of the technology connecting us, relating to one another through ol' school simplicity is disappearing, and I, for one, have dealt with more drama than *Romeo and Juliet* because of it. A dear friend of mine and I were recently texting one another to make plans for a dinner. The exchange went on for a few weeks, because my schedule was so crazy, that

I kept having to change the date. After I changed the date for the third time, I received a text back saying, "You obviously have a lot going on, so let's forget about the dinner." My stomach dropped at her response, because I knew right away she was fed up with the back and forth, so I immediately called her on the phone. She didn't answer, and after leaving a message, I called back later that night, and the night after. Each day that passed, I felt more upset. It took over a week for her to pick up the phone, and when we spoke, she explained that she was frustrated because I didn't call her once during that time, so she figured I didn't really want to meet up and was giving her the runaround. I apologized and admitted that picking up the phone would have made more evident my desire to find a date that worked. Have you ever dealt with something like this? I will guess that you have.

I want to help you avoid similar unnecessary drama.

With the help of *Becoming a Master Communicator*, you will:

1. Understand how you have disengaged from clear-cut human inter-action and how to come back to the distinct and open commu-nication required for all relationships to grow and thrive. You'll also realize how you've disengaged from honest interaction with yourself and how to strengthen that relationship. Once you have a strong relationship with yourself, you create a solid base to build your other connections.

2. Save yourself time, energy, and stress by learning easy, yet power-ful tools that help you become comfortable with getting right to the heart of a communication matter.

3. Take advantage of every opportunity that comes your way by train-ing yourself to ask, "What happens if I *don't* face my fears?"

4. Become an incredible leader in your professional life.

5. Know that being a master communicator is your greatest instrument in establishing true self-confidence, fulfilling relationships, and an extraordinary career.

Through awareness and easy-to-implement practices, you will know when it's best to use technology and when it's best, both personally and professionally, to have a direct conversation to connect effectively.

Our phones and computers are indeed an enormous benefit to us. However, if we depend on them too heavily, they can trap us in the virtual world, and we must never forget we are humans living in the real world. We still need real human contact and real human interaction.

When we sacrifice real human interaction for the sake of artificial intelligence, we become like wild animals roaming only in the confines of a zoo and never running free!

There is a time and a place for humans to roam in both the virtual and real worlds, and understanding that time and place is what becoming a master communicator is all about.

Let's briefly address a few ways in which *"New School Technology"* pulls us away from *"Ol' School Simplicity."*

The first way is through distractions like social media. We can spend endless hours writing Facebook posts or taking ten thousand selfies before getting the perfect one, yet we don't have time to meet a friend in person to catch up or pick up the phone and call them. Let me say that I am speaking from my own experience here, so no judgment on the selfie-taking or texting revolution, but we need to find balance.

The second way is through using texting and emailing as our *primary* means of communicating. This can be dangerous because emails and texts leave lots of room for assumptions, and as you may have heard, when you assume, you make an ass out of you and me.

The third way is through convenience. What makes text messages, email, quick videos, and voice memos so darn attractive is the convenience. Am I right? Why else would everyone use them all the time? Convenient means easier, and if there are two paths to a destination, and one is easier, it is only natural to take that one. The drawback of consistently using one path, though, is that you forget how to navigate the other one when needed. Relying on these faster forms of interaction, we have begun to forget about the other ways to interact. We have convinced ourselves that interacting without a screen as a go-between is more complicated, when, in fact, it's not. We just prefer our interactions to be through that screen. For example, have you ever been impatient with an extended email exchange so you just ended up picking up the phone to call the other person? Me too. Picking up a phone is not more complicated; it's just a matter of preference.

Technology is a beautiful thing, and when used alongside direct human interaction, it can make communication limitless.

To be totally candid here, life can be challenging enough without the added stress of poor and/or impersonal communication, right?

Becoming a Master Communicator provides processes that were created to be as simple as possible, so they can be applied instantly. You will learn what to do, and also what *not* to do, to transform your approach to communication.

I recently completed a powerful course called "The Knowledge Broker Blueprint," taught by the number one personal development coach in the world, Tony Robbins, and self-education entrepreneur Dean Graziosi. In the course, Graziosi teaches an incredible tool called the "Not-To-Do List," where you list the things you engage in daily that move you away from your desired outcome. Seeing what I was wasting time on, right there in front of my eyes, was the exact prompt I needed to no longer do them. On this journey, you, too, will realize the activities you've been engaging in that are distracting you from what you truly want.

When we call ourselves out for spending time on things that don't serve our highest desires, we gain our power back.

Let's look at this book's structure so you will understand the journey we're about to embark upon:

- **Chapter One:** We will discover and explore our communication home. This home is made up of our go-to communication style, which is our most comfortable way of communicating.
- **Chapter Two:** We will break down how new school technology both inhibits and improves our communication.
- **Chapter Three:** We will explore how transparent communication affects our personal and professional relationships, starting with the most important relationship—the relationship with ourselves.
- **Chapter Four:** We will talk about pre-digital technology days and how we can sprinkle in some of the qualities of those days, today.
- **Chapter Five:** We will explore the steps necessary to find balance in our communication methods.
- **Chapter Six:** We will talk about maximizing situations in which we are without direct human contact to continue growing our communication skills.
- **Chapters Seven and Eight:** We will explore easy, tangible practices that help make authentic communication a new habit, while inviting more presence and joy into our lives.
- **Chapter Nine:** We will talk about seizing opportunities by following our intuition and utilizing direct verbal interaction.
- **Chapter Ten:** We will explore taking imperfect action, celebrating ourselves, and deciding how we want to move forward using the tools found in this book!

At the end of each section is a "Reflections Section" with questions to answer that'll give you a chance to ruminate on each section's message. (I also made a printable version of all the Reflections Sections on FreeGiftFromRenee.com so you can have the questions right next to you as you read.) The printable version has more space to write your answers and allows you to save the questions and responses as a standalone to look back to as a refresher after completing the book or anytime.) I understand we are all busy, and some of the questions will appear unnecessary; they may come across as no-brainers or a waste of time, but please trust me—they are necessary and worth your time.

The idea of the Reflections Section was created very strategically with your growth as a priority. Writing after reading helps you to stop and absorb what was read by moving the information from only the mind to the body through the physical action of putting pen to paper. This helps to solidify that knowledge. I picture this process as being like signing a contract—the handwritten signature on the paper makes the deal legit and final.

Writing is also a form of therapy that can help you discover things you didn't know about yourself by revealing some of your hang-ups.

"I write to discover what I know."
— Flannery O'Connor

For those who write in a journal (and if you don't already, I highly suggest it,) how good do you feel after letting the pen flow for a bit? Have you ever looked back at what you wrote and been amazed by it, as if someone else wrote the words, and you are surprised to read what they felt? Me too. Just writing here *about* writing makes me feel a release, like when you've been on your feet all day and you finally sit down!

"Writing is a process. A journey into memory and soul."
— Isabel Allende

Each Reflections Section is there to provide a space for reflection—go figure. The section acts as a mirror reflecting back to you your most vulnerable, raw, and honest self. See, on a regular day, our conscious mind is mostly thinking about the things on our to-do lists. We don't pay much attention to our subconscious, which stores every thought, emotion, trauma, and experience we have ever encountered. When you take the time to respond to the prompts in the Reflections Section, you'll be activating your subconscious mind by being reminded of things you may not have thought about before having to recall them. This process is exceedingly powerful because, in recalling these things, you are becoming aware of them, and awareness is the first step in making positive change.

This book is not a one-time read but rather a guide to refer back to as often as you need. When adding the Reflections Section to *Becoming a Master Communicator*, I envisioned the book serving you, my reader, like a Rick Steves guidebook does for tourists. You can carry it around in your backpack or purse and look to it as often as necessary for a communication check-in.

I have books in my arsenal, like Gabrielle Bernstein's *The Universe Has Your Back* and Jen Sincero's *You Are a Badass*, that I bring with me wherever I go because reading the gems of wisdom inside them immediately brings me back into alignment. I then move on a higher level throughout the day because the quick jolt of inspiration was what I needed to bring me back to my purpose. My hope is *Becoming a Master Communicator* will be a similar source of encouragement for you.

Okay, are you ready? If you haven't downloaded your special gift from FreeGiftFromRenee.com, *now is the time!* Remember, sometimes when it feels too hard or we're too tired, we all need a reminder of why we decided to better ourselves in the first place. This gift will be that daily reminder for you to remain on track to becoming a master communicator. Even when you don't feel like it.

Technology is here to stay, so if we learn to use it to facilitate better communication in our relationships, as opposed to driving a wedge between them, we gain a wonderful advantage. This book will help you maintain harmony in your life that is possible when your phone and computer are working *for* you instead of *controlling* you. Through this illuminating journey, you will become a *master communicator* and thereby empower yourself and strengthen your relationships by balancing two worlds: The world of *"New School Technology"* with *"Ol' School Simplicity."* A win-win for all, baby!

I'm so excited for us to begin, and remember—*you got this!*

Reneé Marino

Chapter One:

DISCOVERING YOUR COMMUNICATION HOME

*"Don't dance around the perimeter of the person you want to be.
Dive deeply and fully into it."*
— Gabrielle Bernstein

A few months ago, I was in my fifth week of one-on-one coaching sessions with Rachel, a client who gave me permission to share her story. Rachel is a beautiful woman in every sense of the word. She has a bright spirit, and like so many of us, is a type-A personality. As a performing artist always looking to better herself and the world, Rachel started her own business helping other performers become experts of their health. Ironically, she put all of her energy and vitality into helping her clients to the point that she had nothing left for herself. Rachel was burnt out physically, emotionally, and spiritually, and as the self-aware woman she is, she knew the only way to fix that was to go within.

Rachel was constantly pushing herself further, harder, and faster, and whether she believed she was a success or failure, she based that belief solely on exterior accomplishments. Throughout our work together, we explored how she communicated with herself and how much of that communication included phrases like, "You're not good enough," "Give more," "Be better," and "What is wrong with you?"

If you're a type-A personality, perhaps you feel that twinge of anxiety upon recognizing these habitual phrases. Rachel realized she was not valuing herself by avoiding dealing with how she really felt, and together we found that this pattern of communication was the same for her external relationships as well. Her go-to communication style for handling conflict was to avoid it. To understand how that pattern developed, we had to dig deeper to find where it began.

Communication is a core part of our being, and just like breathing, it often happens without any thought. Therefore, when we're having a problem in a relationship, we often overlook communication as a possible cause of that problem.

On this particular day, five sessions in, when I asked Rachel how her family communicated when she was growing up, she said, "We never talked about thoughts or feelings. I grew up in a family that was *communication-phobic!*" The second she said the phrase, I got chills throughout my body. I knew her description was so spot-on in pinpointing a characteristic that countless people exhibit, and that it would help so many others put their own experiences into words.

Rachel continued, "Up until my twenties, I didn't even know that feelings were something that *could* be talked about." Can you relate to this? Rachel only knew one style of communication, and that was the one she was accustomed to from her family. Her avoidance pattern caused strain within herself and in all her relationships, especially her cherished ones. Through our digging deep into the foundation of Rachel's exposure to communication, she was able to connect the dots in understanding how and why avoidance was so natural for her. This opened the door to seeing that this was not the *only* way to communicate, but the only way she had been practicing. Now, Rachel realized she could choose another way.

> *Once we become aware that there are other communication styles beyond the ones natural to us, we gain the freedom to try new styles.*

During our time working together in uncovering what habits were holding Rachel back from the fullest expression of her being, she acquired a huge victory that made me so incredibly proud of her. Rachel had a phone conversation with someone she was doing some part-time work for. On the phone, Rachel could tell this person was dissatisfied with how Rachel had taken initiative on a project. When the conversation ended, Rachel felt uneasy from the dissatisfaction she sensed. Her brain wanted to fall into her usual pattern of avoiding and moving on, but through Rachel's new-found awareness of her go-to communication style, and the challenges that it caused throughout her life, she decided to follow her heart and try a new style. Feeling the fear, and before she even knew what she was going to say, Rachel called the person right back to discuss the dissatisfaction.

Yes! This woman whose go-to communication style was avoidance *addressed the situation*! What. A. Win.

After an honest conversation, both agreed they were on different pages and decided to part ways. By understanding her go-to communication style, Rachel was able to choose a different way to communicate, and as a result, save herself time that would have been wasted working somewhere she wasn't meant to work.

The pride I feel over Rachel taking such a huge step is giving me chills again as I write. Rachel is now back to running her business, but this time, she is coaching her clients from a more open and honest place because she is more open and honest with herself.

> *We cannot help others to share their true selves when we are not being true to ourselves!*

How we are most comfortable communicating obviously depends on the situation, but we all have a communication home, which is made up of our go-to communication style—the style of communicating that feels most natural to us. My friend, by discovering your communication home and where it developed, you give yourself a strong starting point from which to cultivate other styles. In turn, you can become a more authentic communicator, and an authentic communicator is a master communicator.

As you read this chapter, focus on discovering *your* communication home. Through my own lived experience, and what I have observed as a communication coach, there are several communication homes. For the sake of simplicity, I've narrowed them down to three main categories of communication homes, with subcategories of the styles that can be tied to each home. Remember, these categories are not judgments of any kind, but rather a framework for understanding your communication habits. Read through each one, and see which resonates with you the most.

1. **The Peace-Keeper**—Preventing confrontation is a priority in their relationships, even if it is at the cost of their own needs or deeper happiness.

   Styles of the Peace-Keeper:

   Avoidance—Doesn't communicate or communicates without addressing what's really going on. May use phrases like, *"I'd rather not argue about it," "I don't want to rock the boat," "It's not worth starting a war over," "That's just how he/she is; I've learned to accept it,"* or *"It's fine."*
   Passive-Aggressive—On the surface, speaks like everything's okay, but then will act in an opposing way, or make targeted statements to suggest otherwise. May use phrases like, *"Oh, don't worry; I don't need help; I'm used to not being able to depend on anyone else,"*

or *"So nice to see you happy for once; usually when it comes to family, we never see a smile from you."*

Mediator—Does everything to diffuse tension in a situation, even if that means taking the blame, to keep everyone happy. Can often use positivity or humor to appease others, and have times of emotional outbursts from keeping true feelings inside too long. May use phrases like, *"Why don't we all take a breath, and come back to this,"* *"I think she's just trying to say that she misses you, but her sadness is coming out in anger,"* or *"Well, I'm sure a disagreement before 8 a.m. is exactly what we wanted for breakfast, huh?"*

2. **The Passion Player**—Getting to the core of what's really going on is a priority in their relationships. Honoring their truth is key.

   Styles of the Passion Player:

   Direct Verbal Interaction—Communicates verbally and straightforward. May use phrases like, *"I'd rather just talk about it,"* *"I'm sorry if I hurt you,"* or *"I was really hurt by what you said."*

   Argument Seeker—No matter the situation, finds a way to make it an argument. May use phrases like, *"Get out of my face right now because I may do something I'll regret,"* or *"I could care less about how you feel because you're the one who made me this mad."*

   Conclusion Jumper—Makes a conclusion before hearing the other person out. May use phrases like, *"Oh, I heard you loud and clear, no need to keep talking,"* or *"I know what you're really trying to say is __."*

3. **The Laid-Back One**—Not being led by emotions is a priority in their relationships. Cool, calm, and collected is how they reside.

   Styles of the Laid-Back One:

Emotional Lack—Communicates directly by stating facts, but without any emotion attached. May use phrases like, *"Yes, of course I am sad this didn't work out, but life is not perfect,"* or *"Just because I'm not jumping for joy doesn't mean I'm not happy to see you."*

Listens, but Doesn't Share—Listens to others wholeheartedly, but never shares their own honest feelings, thoughts, or emotions. May use phrases like, *"Tell me about yourself,"* *"Oh, I'm fine,"* *"There's not much to tell about me,"* or *"I'm kind of boring."*

Steps Back, before Stepping In—Before initiating communication, or reacting to communication, takes time to gather thoughts. May use phrases like, *"I just need a minute,"* *"I'll call you when I'm ready,"* or *"Now is not the right time."*

Once you start to discover your communication home, go a little deeper, asking yourself where the core of that home developed. Was it from the household you were raised in, your closest friend's family you spent time with, a role model, your aunts or uncles, your first boss, or maybe a specific situation that made you begin to doubt yourself and thus shy away from talking much at all?

In a study done at Brigham University, Hart, Newell, and Olsen concluded, "Contrary to recent views suggesting that parents matter little in children's development beyond the influence of genetics and peers, there is ample evidence to suggest that genetics, parents, and even peers all play vital roles in the development of child social and communicative competence."[2]

Trust me, I understand your communication home has been built from a combination of many influences and experiences, but whatever they are, tune into them as we move through this chapter. Any clues that help you

---

2   Hart, C. H., Newell, L. D., & Olsen, S. F. (2003). "Parenting Skills and Social-Communicative Competence in Childhood." In J. O. Greene & B. R. Burleson (eds.). *Handbook of Communication and Social Interaction Skills.* Lawrence Erlbaum Associates Publishers. p. 753–797.

understand why you prefer being behind a screen to communicating face-to-face, or *vice versa*, will only help you balance communication in your personal and professional relationships.

Let's go back to my client Rachel to help make this discovery process clear. She grew up in a "communication-phobic" family that never talked about thoughts or feelings, so as an adult when faced with conflict, she would just turn the other way. Therefore, her communication home was "The Peace-Keeper," with the go-to communication style of *Avoidance*. I know some people who were raised in families that didn't show emotion at all, even over big life events. Subsequently, as adults, their communication home has become "The Laid-Back One," made up of the go-to communication style of *Emotional Lack* because showing any emotion in their relationships is not their strong suit.

There are several people who grew up in an atmosphere of yelling and anger, so now they easily go off the deep end anytime someone says something they do not like. In turn, their communication home is "The Passion Player," with the go-to communication style of the *Argument Seeker.*

Some people were caretakers of parents or grandparents as children and young adults, so they acquired a way of only helping others and focusing on their wants and needs. As a result, their communication home is "The Laid-Back One," made up of the go-to communication style of *Listens, but Doesn't Share.*

Many people grew up immersed in families where everyone was always "nice" to one another. Bubbling just under the surface, though, were all of the untapped feelings of things that needed to be said but never were. Then, those untapped feelings came out in offhanded comments here and there. In turn, these people themselves developed a pattern of appearing like everything is fine and dandy until they say something that reveals otherwise. So, in these cases, their communication home is "The Peace-Keeper," made up of the go-to communication style of *Passive-Aggressive.*

Are you now beginning to understand how this discovery process works? I hope so. There are endless variations in environment and the circumstances people were raised in that shaped their communication home. I used these more direct examples to make it easier for you to understand how your communication home can be developed. Remember, our communication homes are not always a *direct* result of the homes in which we were raised. They can be an *indirect* result of certain situations we faced that had a strong effect on how we view the world, the schools we attended, the people we spent most of our time with besides our family, or a mixture of all these variables.

In the case of my two first cousins, Gina and Erica, even though their mother and father raised them in the same physical home, they could not have more opposite communication homes. We talk about how differently the two of them communicate all the time. If Erica is upset with Gina, she tells her right away and moves on, but Erica only knows if Gina is upset with her, because she can read the look on her face. Otherwise, Gina would never say anything. That is because Gina takes after her father's communication home of "The Peace-Keeper," with the go-to communication style of *Avoidance,* while Erica takes after her mother's communication home, of "The Passion Player," with the go-to communication style of *Direct Verbal Interaction.*

It is also vital to understand that our communication homes all have a starting point, but they can evolve as time moves on, depending on the season we're in within our lives. Once again, looking back to Rachel, her entire life she lived in the communication home of "The Peace Keeper," but through self-awareness and some outside guidance, her location moved to the new home of "The Passion Player."

Let's look at another case. The case of my aunt Jackie. Aunt Jackie is one of the most fun-loving, life-loving, outspoken slices of joy I've ever met. We say we are "partners in crime" because we are both spontaneous, always looking for an adventure, and end up making friends wherever we go because we love to engage in conversation with the people around us.

Aunt Jackie is inclined to tell people her thoughts, feelings, and opinions, even if they aren't warranted, but this was not always the case.

As a young girl, Aunt Jackie grew up in a house with her sister Laura, her brother Donnie, their mom Tessie, and her father John, who was an alcoholic. Day in and day out, she witnessed her father coming home drunk, being angry, and hitting her mother and sister, who spoke back to her father. This situation caused Aunt Jackie to associate speaking up with getting hit, so she never said a peep. To Aunt Jackie, not speaking meant safety. So, for the first twenty years of her life, she was a woman who put her head down, worked hard, and kept to herself until after she was married and her husband—my uncle John—helped her find a new way to communicate.

One day, Uncle John and Aunt Jackie had a marital disagreement. As Uncle John stated his case, he saw a tear roll down Aunt Jackie's cheek. He asked, "Why don't you ever speak up and say something back to me?"

Boy, did he open up a can of worms that day. Aunt Jackie went from never speaking up to never *not* speaking up! Her communication home moved from "The Peace-Keeper," to "The Passion Player," within those short minutes.

Taking the time to discover your communication home is time well spent. By doing so, you gain a better understanding of why you handle situations in your life the way you do. No matter what your go-to communication style is, there is always room for communication improvement, and that is why we're all on this journey together.

Reflections Section: *Discovering Your Communication Home*

- What is your communication home?

_____

_____

_____

_____

- Where do you believe it developed from?

_____

_____

_____

_____

_____

Communication Home in the Workplace

"Communication-the human connection-
is the key to personal and career success."
— Paul J. Meyer

In this part of the chapter, I will share my family life with you and an overview of my years as a performer to illustrate where my own communication home developed from and its role in my work life. Sharing is connecting, so since we are on this journey together, you ought to know more about me as your guide. Also, if you're anything like me, you always want to know more about the person who wrote the book you're reading. I'd love for the stories of my work life to be a reminder for you to look at your current job and recognize the communication style required for that job. Whether you like or dislike that job can be related to the style of communication needed for that line of work and whether that communication style feels comfortable to you or not. Knowing this information can help you narrow down your go-to communication style and, therefore, help you identify your communication home. The same process can be done for your past jobs.

As a girl who grew up in a close-knit, Italian-American family, my mom, dad, brother, and grandmother (who lived with us) would sit around the kitchen table eating, laughing, and sometimes arguing, but most importantly, communicating. We were deeply connected through our endless conversations that helped us learn, question, analyze, and understand things about each other, life, and the ways of the world. If something was bothering me, my parents would always say, "Let's talk about it," and I never fully grasped how monumental those four little words were in shaping my communication home until I got older.

I'll never forget being twelve years old and being cast in an all-girls singing group. I was thrilled when they wanted me as one of their lead singers, but after the first rehearsal, that feeling changed to uneasiness. Throughout the rehearsal, they were trying to change the sound of my voice to be raspier because they said it sounded "too pretty," and they talked about changing my "look" so I'd appear a bit older.

When I got home that day, undeniably upset, my father didn't waste a second before saying, "What's the matter, little shit?"

(Side note: A lot of my friends had nicknames like "sweetheart," "baby doll," or "angel," but my dad's nickname for me was "little shit," and I couldn't have loved it more. In turn, his nickname became "big shit.")

When I explained what went on at rehearsal, he made me feel better immediately by letting me know it was okay to feel upset, and most importantly, to always stay true to myself and be confident in who I was. He reassured me that he supported me in whatever I wanted to do, and when I said I felt I'd be missing out on school and activities by being in the group, he said, "Okay, then, you don't need to be a part of it."

This kind of direct verbal exchange was the norm for me because it was how the five of us operated in my family. Because that style was the basis of our family dynamic and I spent the most time with those four people, my communication home became "The Passion Player," with the go-to communication style of *Direct Verbal Interaction*. It remains the same today.

As a teenage girl, I just figured the way we connected in my family was the standard for all families—until I saw the world by myself as an independent young woman.

The first time I left home for an extended period was when I went away to Wagner College and lived on campus. Although I lived in the dorms, the college was close enough to my hometown that I could go home on the weekend if I needed to, or my family could come up and take me out to dinner. When I say *could*, I mean *would* take me out to dinner because our lives centered, and still center, around food. Deciding to live at school was one of the greatest decisions of my life because it let me stand on my own two feet away from the beautiful bubble of where I came from, in a world full of individuals from all over the globe.

During this chapter of my life, I met so many wonderful people, some of whom became my best friends, and what I learned was this: Not everyone sits around the kitchen table talking openly about thoughts, feelings, and ideas with their families. We are all from different cultures, nationalities, circumstances, religions, and countries, and that means how we communicate is different as well.

My best friend Chris and I get such a kick out of the memory of the first day we met in college because my communication style of *Direct Verbal Interaction* was in full effect. I walked right up to him and said, "Hi, I'm Renée; so nice to meet you," and then gave him a big, tight hug. Chris was not used to that style of communication, so he thought I was nuts!

I began to see that, because everyone had their own communication style, my style was not always the "right" one. Sometimes, my roommate didn't want to talk when something was bothering her, so I needed to know when to step back and say nothing at all.

Being surrounded by so many diverse people with diverse backgrounds made those four years some of the best of my life. They were the stepping-stones to expanding my awareness of myself and the world beyond where I grew up. This awareness continued to grow through my work and travel, which began immediately after graduation. The day after graduation to be exact—May 22, 2004.

I was on a plane to Biloxi, Mississippi, to begin working as the lead singer in a casino show called "Heatwave." I'll never forget seeing my picture on a billboard on the interstate and thinking that meant I had *made it*. For three months, I sang and danced my butt off doing two shows a night, six days a week, with meet and greets after each show, and I loved every single second of it.

The day I got my first paycheck, I called my mom from the balcony of my hotel room to say, "Do you see why I do this? I just got paid to do what I love!" At that moment, I viscerally understood the quote from Confucius that I chose for all of my college application essays to express why I wanted to major in musical theatre: "Choose a job you love, and you will never have to work a day in your life."

After three and a half months, my time singing and dancing in Biloxi was up, so I moved back home with my family in New Jersey, and once there, I began auditioning in New York City for all various kinds of performance jobs. The jobs I went in for ranged from regional theatre shows, cruise ships, tours, and Broadway musicals to Las Vegas shows, commercials, music videos, television shows, and films.

Meanwhile, I worked as a substitute teacher by day for the middle schools in my town, as well as my alma mater high school (which was so trippy because I had been a student there just four years prior). I quickly learned how important my communication home was to my livelihood, especially as a young substitute teacher. If I wanted cooperation and respect, I needed to verbalize, transparently and authoritatively, what I expected from the students while remaining relatable. In other words, I had to be a master communicator as the leader of the classroom. This job put my communication home, "The Passion Player," to work, and it made me appreciate that direct verbal interaction came naturally to me.

After hustling in and out of the city from September through May of 2005, my next traveling adventure came when I booked the twenty-fifth anniversary tour of *Cats* and toured all over North America for a year. Nothing helps you recognize communication homes more than touring with the same group of people for one entire year. We were on the bus together, shoulder-to-shoulder, for up to fourteen hours a day. To boot, we were on stage together, in rehearsals together, and in the same living quarters together. We call it the "tour bubble" because that tour becomes your own little world. Through this unique experience, I got to understand the ways we all handled new experiences, disagreements, and issues, such as something feeling dangerous on stage, based on our communication homes. On several occasions, arguments would ensue because of a conflict of communication homes. Here's an example: There were two bus buddies, and one person had a communication home of "The Peace Keeper," with the go-to communication style of *Passive Aggressive,* and the other a home of the "The Passion Player," with the go-to style of the *Argument Seeker.* Person A, "The Peace Keeper," was feeling annoyed by person B, "The Passion Player," because person B was keeping person A awake due to the loud music that came through his headphones. Person A, in his *Passive Aggressive* style, acted completely normal to person B, but was overheard by person B making a snide remark to some other friends about being kept awake by person B's music. In his *Argument Seeker* style, when person B heard this, fireworks went off as he shared his anger with person A, and person A went into defensive mode.

Situations similar to this one happened all the time. This up-close-and-personal tour life helped me understand that our communication homes influence how we engage with the people in our lives.

After *Cats,* I traveled with the national tour of Disney's *High School Musical* for nine months in 2007 and then *Jersey Boys* for a year and a half. So, after being on the road for three years and three months, I decided to head back to the NYC audition scene, so I could be in the place of possibilities to make my childhood dream of performing on Broadway come true. When I decided not to renew my last contract on tour, many people thought I was crazy to leave such a great job with great pay, but I didn't listen because even though tour life was rewarding, I knew it was not my heart and soul's deepest desire.

I want to bring up an essential point here. My ability to make career choices came down to using my go-to communication style of *Direct*

Verbal Interaction to communicate not just with others but with myself too. By asking questions and keeping an open dialogue with me, myself, and I, I could tune out others' noise, travel on my path, and keep my focus strong as I worked toward making my childhood dream come to life.

Here is a little tip for you:

No matter where your communication home is located, practicing honest intrapersonal communication lays the groundwork for becoming a master communicator.

We will explore intrapersonal communication in Chapter Three, but until then, know that once you have great communication with yourself, you set the standard for every other relationship you have.

Back in the Big Apple, at the beginning of 2010, I pounded the pavement for a few months, sometimes doing several auditions in one day, until I got an unexpected surprise. I was at a callback for a regional theatre show when the casting director called me into his office. He happened to be the same casting director for the Broadway revival of *West Side Story*, which I had auditioned for months prior and made it down to the last few women. He asked me if I sang "soprano," and when I said yes, he said, "We need you as a replacement for *West Side Story* on Broadway. Go to the theatre tonight!" My response was, "I think I just peed my pants!" Just a few days later, before my rehearsals were even complete and much sooner than I was scheduled to, I had my Broadway debut on the stage of the Palace Theatre.

My Broadway debut with *West Side Story* was a phenomenal adventure. I had the joy of playing various Shark and Jet roles until the book writer/director Arthur Laurents asked me to take over the part of "Rosalia," who gets to sing the iconic song, "America" alongside Anita. I was with the show for the last eight months it was on Broadway, until it closed on January 2, 2011, and a few months later, I began rehearsals for an original Broadway musical called, *Wonderland.*

The show had played on Broadway for only one month when I got a phone call on a Tuesday telling me the show was closing in five days! Truth be told, I didn't know how to react at first. I was so stunned that I didn't know whether to laugh or cry—so I did both. Using my go-to communication style of *Direct Verbal Interaction* intrapersonally, I let myself feel whatever I felt and honored those feelings. I didn't ignore the feelings, or push them away; I experienced them. By doing this, I was able to release those feelings, and begin to look forward to what was next. After doing several workshops (work-through sessions of creating new musicals or plays, with a performance of some numbers and scenes without a full-scale production), I made my way back to Broadway, this time with the musical *Chaplin*. When *Chaplin* closed after six months, I was over the moon to join the Broadway cast of *Jersey Boys*, that led me to my first on-screen role in the movie *Jersey Boys*, which filmed in Los Angeles. I have dedicated an entire chapter to sharing every part of my film experience with you, but I want to give you this golden nugget right now. Being a part of this major motion picture was a precise result of communicating from my home—"The Passion Player"—and using my go-to communication style of *Direct Verbal Interaction*, but more on this later....

When I completed filming, my boyfriend Michael asked me to marry him, and we moved out to Los Angeles from 2014-2017. Being in LA, immersed in the television and film world, was such an exhilarating time. I played my first guest star role on a Fox TV sitcom pilot, did a commercial, had the honor of walking and being interviewed on several red carpets, wrote and performed my one-woman show, was in my first two-person play, was a singer at the El Capitan Theatre in Hollywood, and played two incredible roles in two different musicals. Michael and I loved our time on the West Coast and the chosen family we acquired, but in the spring of 2017, we realized we were ready to move back to the East Coast to buy a home and be close to our family.

I also realized I really missed the Broadway community, so as soon as we got back home, I started auditioning and was cast in the final workshop of *Pretty Woman: The Musical*. As a huge fan of the movie, I was thrilled when asked to continue as part of the cast when it moved to Broadway. I not only performed in the ensemble but was also the dance captain and assistant to the choreographer. Being on both sides of the table—the performing and creative sides—was a new endeavor that I immensely relished. As the dance captain, I had to teach the choreography to new cast members, run rehearsals, run auditions, and give verbal notes to the cast, so the job relied solely on direct verbal communication skills. In this case, my go-to communication style was an excellent match for the one needed for my job.

From *Pretty Woman*, I was ready to pivot in my career, and with my deep passion for communication, I became a communication coach. When you really think about it, it makes complete sense that someone with a communication home of "The Passion Player," with the go-to communication style of *Direct Verbal Interaction*, would choose a profession that helps others become comfortable with directly and authentically communicating.

Our communication homes really do play a role in every aspect of our lives, from how we connect to one another, to what line of work we enjoy. When I was in high school, I had to get a minor surgery, and I spoke to the anesthesiologist beforehand. He said something so funny yet so poignant in relation to our communication homes. He said, "I don't like talking to people very much, and that's why I became an anesthesiologist. So, I can put people right to sleep!" Makes sense, huh?

Maybe you're working at a job you really dislike. Take the time to identify what communication style is required for this job; doing so could help you understand what your communication home is *not* to get you closer to understanding what your communication home *is*. Alternatively, if you're in your ideal job, identify what communication style causes you to thrive in this area; this can be a great indication of your home. Remember, there is not always a direct relation of your work to your communication home, but it can be a sign pointing you in the right direction!

Reflections Section: *Communication Home in the Workplace*

- Do you like or dislike your current job?

_____

_____

_____

_____

- What communication style is required for that job?

_____

_____

_____

_____

- Do you see a correlation between how you feel about your job and the communication style needed for that job?

_____

_____

_____

_____

- If so, how does this help point to your communication home?

_____

_____

_____

*Remember, you can download the printable version of all the Reflections Sections at FreeGiftfromRenee.com.

Any information we can accumulate to help us better understand ourselves by understanding how and why we choose to interact with one another the way we do is valuable data for our journey to becoming a master communicator. Discovering your communication home and what go-to style makes up that home starts your journey on solid footing. Do not stress if you feel like you don't know what yours is yet, because merely understanding that you *have* a communication home and a go-to style that makes up that home, in and of itself, has made you more self-aware. Take a deep breath and know that you are not alone on this journey. As we move forward, you will gain more communication clarity, which will make your home and go-to style more apparent. In the next chapter, we will break down how new school technology both inhibits and improves our communication, so pat yourself on the back for being honest with yourself in this chapter, and keep that honesty going, my friend!

Chapter Two

NEW SCHOOL TECHNOLOGY (LIFE AS WE KNOW IT)

"To be clear, technology is a vital part of progress and being limitless. It allows us to do everything from connecting to learning, making our lives that much more convenient. But it is possible that we consume digital technology at a rate that even its creators would find extreme. Much of the technology available to us is so new that we don't know the level at which we need to control our interaction with it."
— Jim Kwik

How Technology Inhibits Communication

This chapter is all about seeing both sides of the coin: how technology inhibits our communication, and how technology improves our communication. If we are only swept away by the magic of new school technology, which is quite easy to let happen, then we can unconsciously put ourselves in a position of being totally dependent on that technology.

This dependence, in turn, can create challenges in how we connect with one another.

Let's use the analogy of an antibiotic prescribed when we're sick. If we take more than the dosage suggested, we can end up doing more harm than good to our bodies. Hence, when we receive the bottle of antibiotics, a piece of paper comes along with it that lists the side effects to make us aware of them. Well, the cons (versus pros) of technology discussed in the first part of this chapter are the *side effects* of a higher dosage of new school technology than necessary. Please do your best not to feel defensive if you are a technology lover, as am I. These cons are not written to point fingers, but rather to indicate the places where some side effects have taken over. Remember, our end goal is to find balance in our communication, so we have to see the full scope of the pros and cons of new school technology; then we can consciously choose how we communicate. This journey is all about love, my friend, so know that everything written is from a place of love.

The paradox with current innovations is they were created to make our lives easier, yet we often find ourselves more stressed. We love our fancy touchscreen refrigerator, except when it breaks down. Then we have to buckle up and be prepared to sit for a while as we endure the pain of trying to get an actual human being on the phone when we call the repair service line.

Dealing with the computer that says, "You can talk to me like a person. I understand complete sentences" is enough to drive you insane. Every time you have to repeat yourself because the automated voice on the other end hears background noise and says, "I did not understand," the anxiety rises a little bit higher, and by the time you have a real person on the phone, all you want to do is scream!

Oh, but it doesn't end there because once you talk to a person, they put you on hold to connect you to a different department, and the call disconnects. All of a sudden, you find yourself longing for the days when you had a simple refrigerator with no bells and whistles, with your peace intact. With so many gadgets that are supposed to make our lives more effortless, we can't understand why we feel anxious and on edge. When I hear, "You can talk to me *like* a person," I often ask, "Well, then why not have a *real* person?"

Let's open our awareness to explore how all of these technological advances have affected us. When I think about the role these advances play in our lives, I envision the *taijitu* symbol representing the Chinese concept of yin and yang. According to the *Ancient History Encyclopedia*, "The principle of Yin and Yang is that all things exist as inseparable and contradictory opposites, for example, female-male, dark-light, and old-young. Neither pole is superior to the other and, as an increase in one brings a corresponding decrease in the other, a correct balance between two poles must be reached in order to achieve harmony."[3]

We need both yin and yang, just like we need new school technology and ol' school simplicity to achieve communication harmony. When there is too much of one or the other, complications follow. I'm sure most of us wish life was only full of happy times and days of pure sunshine and rainbows, but those moments wouldn't be as fulfilling if we didn't have the contrast of the clouds and rain.

The yin and yang concept represents the perfection of the imperfection of life. As a performing artist, I had to miss many special moments with my family and friends like holidays, birthdays, and weddings because I didn't have a nine-to-five job. "Yin." On the other hand, I was extremely fortunate to have a job that was also my hobby. I loved what I did and didn't take one second for granted, knowing that not everyone gets to do what they love as their job. "Yang."

Even though my work was incredible, it wasn't perfect—I sacrificed "normal" family life and had to find alternative moments to spend with my loved ones. Although it wasn't always easy, I made it a priority to find those moments. It was my way of restoring equilibrium. If I only focused

---

3   Cartwright, Mark. "Yin and Yang." *Ancient History Encyclopedia*. Last modified May 16, 2018. https://www.ancient.eu/Yin_and_Yang/.

on work, letting my personal life fall by the wayside, my life would have been out of balance. When it comes to the use of artificial intelligence, that same imbalance is happening.

We are using fewer of the basic skills and qualities inherent in our human brain because we're too busy using an artificial brain.

The time has come, my friend, to go through this list together and see the effects an over-reliance on new school technology has had on us.

1. **We Have Expectations, Instead of Appreciation.** With the power of the World Wide Web, and the devices that we possess, we're accustomed to having what we need or want, at lightning speed. Because this magnitude of convenience has become standard for us, there is always an expectation of receiving that standard. Then, when something gets in the way of what we expect, we may feel aggravated, anxious, angry, or slighted. This happens because we have taken for granted what we have, instead of appreciating what we have. We expect our computer to boot up immediately, our email to reach its destination, and our text to make sense without punctuation. Then, when these things don't go perfectly, we throw tantrums. Have you ever cursed your computer in deep irritation because a webpage didn't load in less than ten seconds? Me too. How about having a fit when the newest iPhone was on back order and you had to wait three whole months to get the new phone? Don't worry; you're not alone. Getting irritated by these very minor annoyances shows we're not taking the time to appreciate how lucky we are to have the internet or the amazing technology behind that new phone.

   When it comes to the use of technology in our communication with one another, the same expectation is occurring. With our smart-phones constantly on hand, there is an expectation that we must always be available and that others must be available to us. In *The Distracted Mind*, Gazzaley and Rosen point out:

> The same radical change in our expectations has extended to all communication modalities. If our text message is not responded to immediately, we attribute motivations to the recipient—'She must be mad at me'—or if we comment on someone's Facebook post and he doesn't immediately respond or, at the least, 'like' our comment, we get miffed and feel rebuffed. As more of our personal communications move from the real world to the virtual world, more opportunities arise for others to not meet our expectations.[4]

Think about times when you have placed motivations on your text messages' recipients because their responses weren't arriving as fast as you expected. How about a time when a friend didn't pick up your video call when you had something pressing to tell them, and you decided that meant they were ignoring you, so you became angry with them? Having these expectations can certainly cause strain in our relationships because when our expectations are not met, we attach meaning to why they aren't. Those meanings are often different from the actual reasons. The act of expecting also makes us focus on what's missing. This puts us and our relationships in a state of distress, by overlooking all that is available to us. It's like walking into a restaurant for dinner with a friend you haven't seen in a long time, and the first question you ask is, "Do you have Wi-Fi?" When they say no, your immediate reaction is to say, "Thank you," and then leave to find another restaurant. Meanwhile, instead of appreciating the limited time you have to catch up with your friend, you're wasting that limited time by being in a state of

---

4   Gazzaley, Adam and Larry D. Rosen. *The Distracted Mind: Ancient Brains in a High-Tech World*. Cambridge, MA: MIT Press, 2016.

expecting to find Wi-Fi. By realizing this pattern of expectation, we can transform it by trading our expectations, for appreciation, as Tony Robbins says.

Reflections Section: *We Have Expectations, Instead of Appreciation*

- What is a situation or situations when your technology expectations caused you distress or a relationship of yours distress? (Do not feel ashamed or embarrassed because the more real you are, the more real your positive changes will be. Dig deep.)

_____

_____

_____

_____

_____

2. **We Don't Make Small Talk.** Ah, small talk. One of my favorite things to take part in. I cannot tell you how many times I've experienced the following situation. I'm waiting in line at a store or sitting in the waiting room of a doctor's office, and I say hello to the person next to me. They look at me like I have three heads, and then go back to their faces in the phone, and I just want to yell out, "Are you kidding me? I just said hello. I didn't ask you for five-hundred dollars!" As you can tell, this behavior deeply bothers me because it represents a decline in human connection. It's like people have literally forgotten how to casually interact with each other, and small talk is becoming a lost art. Let's be frank here. Any idle time that we have nowadays is spent with our phones, right? What happened to the days when making friendly conversation with the people around you felt natural? The days when you found

yourself having the most inspiring talk with a stranger, or when you realized you had mutual friends with the person sitting next to you? How about when small talk with the person waiting in line next to you developed into deep talks with the person you fell in love with?

We are denying ourselves opportunities by always being glued to our phones instead of staying open and available.

When I hear friends say, "Oh, I can't meet anybody when I go out anymore; that's why I *have* to do online dating," I say, "Well, that's because when you're out somewhere you're not really out; you're in your phone, and that doesn't give off the energy of 'Hey, I'm looking to meet someone great!'" Pick that head up and smile because you never know what great relationship could be one table away from you at the restaurant!

Reflections Section: *We Don't Make Small Talk*

- List two times when either you or another person initiated small talk and something positive came out of the conversation. How did you feel afterward?

_____

_____

_____

_____

_____

3. **Writing Skills Have Declined.** As part of my research on this topic, I spoke to more than fifty parents and teachers in person, and I also posted the following question on both Facebook and Instagram: "Do you find that children today have trouble taking notes

well, or writing clearly because they're used to shortcut spelling from texting and social media?" Ninety-seven percent responded "Yes!" The few who said "No" explained that they made a conscious effort to teach their children traditional handwriting at home through card and letter writing as a means to offset this potential setback. Between social media, texting, work in the school system being mostly done on computers, or classes being completely virtual, as one teacher commented, "Writing pen to paper takes practice and skill, and it's not done as much these days." When I posed the same question to my sister-in-law, who has been a high school guidance counselor for nine years, she said:

> One million percent yes, it's a huge concern. Another cause of their struggle with writing is the distraction from their cell phones. They'll start writing, and two minutes later their phone will ding, and then they're completely thrown off. Because of this problem, I teach a program that focuses specifically on how to take notes, stay organized, and write in an agenda book.

Many of us cannot structure a well-thought out sentence or letter simply because we are mostly typing now, and we can let an electronic application like Grammarly fix our errors for us. I understand some of you may be thinking, *Well, why would we need to know how to write then?* Because, when required, you want to be able to clearly and correctly present the necessary information in writing. If you were interviewing someone for a job and they were educated and had the required skills, but could not write a basic paragraph about why they were the best person for the job, would you want to hire them? How about if they couldn't even type a proper email or document? The decline in traditional handwriting has carried over to our ability to properly type an email or letter as well. Just yesterday, my husband Michael received an email from a gentleman he was potentially going to work with. A few days earlier, after talking with the man and his team, Michael had been optimistic about the possible partnership. Once he opened the email, his optimism turned to doubt because it read as if it were written by a five-year-old. There was no greeting, lots of shortcut spelling, misspelled words, no punctuation, no closing, and the words chosen for the body of the letter made the tone of the letter feel aggressive. Michael was taken aback and asked me to read the email to see if he was overreacting. When I did, I agreed with him completely. To me, this man should have been putting his best foot forward by writing an email that represented his professionalism. If he couldn't take the time to write a proper, respectful email, it indicated to me that he did not take pride in how he related to business associates or anyone else for that matter. Michael said, "None of us is perfect, but this email showed no effort, which makes me believe this is the same effort he puts into his work." Michael decided not to move forward with the partnership and felt very confident in his decision.

How and what you write is a representation of you.

We want to give ourselves every chance to succeed in whatever endeavor we pursue. Having the capability to write well—whether it's a vital document, clear notes, or a heart-centered letter—is a powerful tool for success and strengthens our ability to type more accurately too. By completely replacing our writing with typing, and not practicing the technique of putting pen to paper, we are losing a very valuable skill.

4. **We Don't Sit With Ourselves.** Purely stated, we can easily avoid ourselves and what is really going on within because we have

these great little toys to distract us. Why would we need to sit and think about emotions we'd prefer to suppress when we can play a game on our iPads, or scroll away on social media platforms from our phones? We use our digital devices for just about everything, which is a tricky situation because some of those things help us and some of them hurt us. For instance, isn't it funny that many of us use our phones as alarm clocks (which helps us), but the phone also keeps us awake because our brains are wired from the blue light (which hurts us)?

As humans, we are very good at immersing ourselves in countless behaviors and situations, like overeating, drinking, fighting, overworking, watching television for hours, or spending most of our time with electronic devices so we can run away from what we need to handle.

> *"Your willingness to look at your darkness*
> *is what empowers you to change."*
> — Iyanla Vanzant

These devices make escaping our innermost selves quite effortless, because with only the touch of a button, our focus can move from inside our beings to inside the virtual world. There, we can take part in a slew of activities we believe will make us feel better, yet they make us feel worse. Can you identify with this? We don't want to feel our feelings, so instead, we look at everyone else's pages on social media and compare our real life to their collection of perfectly filtered photos and videos. And then, guess what? We feel badly about ourselves! As much as we may not want to hear this truth, we must listen if we want to begin the process of healing. The only way out of our pain and uncomfortable emotions is on the other side of feeling them.

We can run as fast as we want, but until we stop repressing and start addressing, the shadows will follow us in every chapter of our lives.

What we think of as the antidote to suffering (distracting ourselves with television, social media, video games, etc.) is actually causing more suffering. By not taking the time to tap into who we are, what we want, and what we need to work on, we miss out on the wholeness of our being. This wholeness is precisely what provides the solid ground for strong external relationships to be created, so the time has come to put the gadgets down and sit with ourselves. The virtual world will always be there, but connect with it after you've spent some time traveling within first.

Reflections Section: *We Don't Sit with Ourselves*
- What feelings/traumas/situations have you been avoiding?

_____

_____

_____

_____

_____

- List activities you take part in that distract you from going within.

_____

_____

_____

5. **We Have Lost Our Ability to Focus.** Through the variety of technological gadgets that we have, paired with the endless information and stimulation that each one provides, it is no wonder that

focusing on any one thing for too long can be a challenge. In an article from *Technology and Society Magazine*, Raquel Benbunan-Fich shares:

> When attention is divided, no task is the beneficiary of the full extent of our abilities. Partial attention diminishes one's capacity to work well and use all of the mental resources in the pursuit of the goal associated with the task. As a result of juggling multiple tasks, wrong decisions are made, incorrect information is conveyed, and mistakes are committed. With the illusion of multitasking productivity comes the risk of forewarned underperformance.[5]

This one resonates with me deeply because there are days when I'll be writing an email on my laptop, with my phone next to me on the desk. The phone will light up telling me someone has sent me a direct message on LinkedIn. Before I know it, I have left the email half-written in front of me with my phone in hand, where I've drifted from answering that direct message to answering a text message, and somehow forty-five minutes go by before I get back to the email! Can you relate? What we are able to see, learn, and do, because of new school technology is boundless, but the loss of our full focus and full exploration as we're seeing, learning, and doing becomes a consequence. This loss in ability to focus directly ties in to how we communicate because fully connecting with someone or even yourself takes focus. If that focus is split, I know you can guess how strong that communication and, in turn, relationship will be.

---

5   Benbunan-Fich, Raquel. (2012). "The Ethics and Etiquette of Multitasking in the Workplace." *Technology and Society Magazine.* 31 (2012): 15-19.

Reflections Section: *We Have Lost Our Ability to Focus*

- List a time when you struggled with focusing. Be specific in recalling all of the different things you were doing at that time.

_____

_____

_____

_____

- What did you feel emotionally and mentally as you struggled to focus?

_____

_____

_____

_____

- List a time when your split focus caused a problem in a relationship of yours. (This also includes times when you haven't focused enough on yourself, and as a result, you felt less than your best, burned out, or neglected.)

_____

_____

_____

_____

- List a time when someone's split focus toward you caused a problem in your relationship.

_____

_____

_____

_____

6. **We Have Lost Our Ability to Listen.** Listening is one of the most crucial parts of communicating with one another, and the loss of this makes me so sad. True listening requires one's undivided attention, but with the abundance of diversions that our devices offer, our attention becomes quite divided. As Sherry Turkle writes in her book, *Alone Together*:

> Mobile technology has made each of us 'pauseable.' Our face-to-face conversations are routinely interrupted by incoming calls and text messages. In the world of paper mail, it was unacceptable for a colleague to read his or her correspondence during a meeting. In the new etiquette, turning away from those in front of you to answer a mobile phone or respond to a text has become close to the norm. When someone holds a phone, it can be hard to know if you have that person's attention.[6]

So, between our decreased attention spans, and our minds being programmed to wait for the sound of a notification, how could we fully listen?

My friend, listen up about listening:

---

6   Turkle, Sherry. *Alone Together: Why We Expect More From Technology and Less from Each Other.* New York: Basic Books, 2011. p. 161.

Like Pavlov's dogs conditioned to salivate when they heard the bell, we are becoming conditioned to check out of what we're doing the instant we hear the ding of a notification.

How many times have you been telling a friend a story and, as you're talking, they are going back and forth from looking at you to looking at their phone? Then, all of a sudden, you feel a complete disconnect, and the desire to finish your story goes away? Oh, boy, if you're anything like me, you've dealt with this a lot. The worst is when you're emotionally struggling and you need a friend's complete attention. The tears are flowing, you can barely catch your breath, and out of nowhere your friend begins answering a text!

The road goes both ways, though, my friend. How many times have you been the one "half-listening?" How often have you just *had* to look at your phone for one minute to check if your ex posted any new pictures on Facebook, or have you been quietly sitting in anticipation of the story to finish so you could swipe on Bumble? Take the time to really think about this because a little soul searching goes a long way here!

I'd like to bring forth one more observation about listening.

"Most people do not listen with the intent to understand; they listen with the intent to reply."
— Stephen Covey

Stephen Covey hits the nail on the head with this quote, because due to an inability to focus for very long, many people treat listening as waiting for the other person to finish speaking so they can start. This leads to people talking *at* each other, instead of *to* each other, and that never makes for good communication. Have you ever been a part of or noticed a conversation with opposing beliefs going on, and there is no seeking to understand at all because each person just wants to state their case and "win"? They feel confident telling why their view is the "right" one because they have this handy-dandy machine of information in their hand to back them up with evidence in seconds to support their claim. When you begin to listen actively and entirely, you give as well as receive a contribution. You give respect by offering an open forum for the other person/people to be heard, and you gain an opportunity to receive knowledge, inspiration, understanding, or a new perspective you didn't have previously. Right now, let's all do a conscious reset of how we listen to one another. Just by being mindful of the habits we've picked up, we can keep ourselves in check the next time we're in a conversation.

Listening skills make us great communicators, so we shortchange ourselves and our relationships when we lose them.

Reflections Section: *We Have Lost Our Ability to Listen*

- List an instance when someone was "half-listening" to you. How did you feel when this happened?

_____

_____

_____

_____

- Recall an instance when *you* were the one "half-listening." What do you think you could have done to make yourself more available?

_____

_____

_____

_____

- List a time when you were in a conversation with someone, and you could tell they were not listening to you but waiting to jump in, so they could speak. How did that make you feel?

_____

_____

_____

_____

- List a time when you were the one already planning what you were going to say, and waiting to jump in to speak. (By calling yourself out, this will help make you more mindful the next time you're in a conversation.)

_____

_____

_____

_____

7. **We've Developed Keyboard Confidence**

   Do you find when writing a post on Facebook or ranting on Twitter about your political stance that your truest feelings somehow flow out in the perfect number of characters? You can write all day, arguing back and forth with a person with an opposing view, exchanging words of disdain without a second thought? Yet, if that person were right in front of you, you would be reluctant to share the same deep-rooted feelings? Well, my friend, this is what I call "Keyboard Confidence." Keyboard confidence is the raw, unfiltered, unapologetic confidence that is only present behind a screen and through the fingers.

As I write about this, the visual that pops into my head is that of the Wizard from the movie *The Wizard of Oz*. When hiding behind his "mask" of the manufactured voice and persona, he was, in fact, the "Great and Powerful," until the curtain of that persona was pulled back and he had nothing to hide behind. We then saw him for who he really was—an insecure "humbug," as Dorothy said.

Our digital screens have become our masks.

We hide behind our masks so often that we've convinced ourselves the masks *are* us. Then, when the masks are removed—when we have to move through the world in our own skin—we become insecure just like the Wizard.

Have you ever experienced a friend you know on a very deep level becoming an entirely different person on social media? I've had moments when I had to look twice at a friend's post because I wondered who wrote the post and what they had done with my friend. Things were written that I *knew* my friend would never acknowledge feeling, much less say in person.

The beauty of social media is that it provides a platform for our right to free speech and expression, and that's wonderful, and also why we love it so much. We feel safe in the realm of the internet because we are literally behind a screen and don't have to face our "opponents," or even friends, for that matter. In turn, we allow our most genuine feelings to arise. The problem lies, though, in the inability to express those same feelings when the screen is gone, and we are faced with actual human beings.

Keyboard confidence is, in a nutshell, kind of like this: You and your friend Nicole go out for dinner every Saturday night, after making plans the Wednesday before. For the past few weeks, you've been going to the same Mexican restaurant because you both love the nachos. When you call her Wednesday, you say, "I can't stop thinking about those nachos. Do you want to go back on Saturday?" Nicole takes a second to respond, and you can hear some hesitation when she says, "Sure, I can do that." You respond with, "Nicole, let's go wherever you want. Seriously, I'm cool with going somewhere new. What are you feeling?" She continues to say she's down for the Mexican restaurant and then moves on with the conversation. Later, you see a post on her Twitter page posted ten minutes after your phone conversation. The post says, "Sometimes I feel like I'm still a child with everyone else around me as my parent. For once, I'd like to make my own decisions." Immediately, your stomach drops because you instinctually feel this post is about you. You pick up the phone and say, "Hey, Nicole, I just saw your tweet. Was that about me and picking the restaurant?" You can tell she is stumped and begins mumbling as she searches for what to say. You continue, "I told you to pick the restaurant, so if you didn't want to eat Mexican again, why wouldn't you just say that?" She says, "I don't know why I didn't say something. I'm just having a bad day, so I'm sorry for posting that." You get off the phone feeling deceived about how she could passive-aggressively write a post but not say upfront how she felt. I admit this example is pretty laughable, but do you understand what I am trying to say here?

Here's one more example. Your sibling is extremely shy and reserved. They would rather be stuck on an elevator for seven hours than confront someone. One day, you go on your sibling's Facebook page and see a long back-and-forth disagreement with a stranger about a recent event in the news. The argument is very intense, and your sibling is calling this other person harsh names because they disagree with your sibling's view. The more you read, the more you feel like you're in the Twilight Zone. This is your sibling who barely makes small talk and would never dare speak like that to someone in person, so what the heck is going on? They were simply acting out with *Keyboard Confidence*, and your duty as a sibling is to make them aware of that.

Yes, we all have freedom of speech and expression. We can write whatever we choose, but if our goal is to become master communicators, then we need to have the confidence we have when typing on a keyboard to carry over to our in-person conversations. A way to cultivate this habit is to ask yourself one small question before you post, email, or text: "Would I feel comfortable talking about this in person?" If the answer is no, grab a journal, have a cathartic writing session, and let yourself jot down every thought and feeling. Then go back to the keyboard and write only what you would be ready to discuss face-to-face. Contrarily, if the answer is yes, then post away. Remember this:

Being authentic is one of the greatest gifts we can give ourselves and others. When we have only keyboard confidence, we're not being truly authentic.

Sure, the Wizard seemed big and intimidating behind his mask, but he never actually became the "Great and Powerful Oz" until he owned up to who he truly was. It's funny that only when the mask was *removed* could he help Dorothy and her friends. Let's all be great and powerful and remove those masks, shall we?

Reflections Section: *We've Developed Keyboard Confidence*

- Have you ever posted something on social media or anywhere in the public eye that you *know* you would not have the nerve to say in person? Take a few moments to look back at your social media posts or blogs and get really honest.

_____

_____

- If you have made such posts, write two of those down. Then next to each original post, rephrase and rewrite it how you would have the confidence to say it in person.

Original Post   Updated Post

_____   _____

_____   _____

_____   _____

_____   _____

_____

How Technology Improves our Communication

*"We often take for granted the very things
that most deserve our gratitude."*
— Cynthia Ozick

Have you ever *really* taken a moment to stop and think about all the ways technology has added convenience, opportunity, and power to your life? If not, let's do so together. When we remind ourselves of the luxuries we have, we cannot help but be grateful, and if there is one feeling that we want to lean into, it is gratitude. Gratitude is the safest, most organic, most effective medicine for any type of fear we may experience, and the best part is we don't need a doctor to write the prescription. We can write one for ourselves.

Through gratitude, we come back to the center of our spirit, and from that center, we tap into our truest selves. When we function from our truest selves, we move from our heads and into our hearts, and that naturally opens our eyes to the blessings all around us. By being cognizant of all that technology gives us, we move away from taking advantage of it, and we step into the wonder of acknowledgment.

As a child, one of my favorite cartoons was *The Jetsons.* The show was set in the year 2062, and as a little girl, I was mesmerized by the family's cool, futuristic lifestyle. They had a robot housekeeper named Rosie, flying cars, and a machine called the "Foodarackacycle" that made any food they wanted with the push of a button. (This is still a dream machine of mine!) They had a flat screen television, a moving walkway inside their home, a robotic vacuum, a talking alarm clock, and video phones where they could see one another and talk through a screen. Sound familiar?

I remember watching the show and daydreaming about the time when I could live like the Jetsons. We're not even in 2062 yet, but in many ways, we are already beyond what those writers imagined when they wrote the show. We are in the future, my friend, and it is astonishing! I, for one, feel as fortunate as the Jetsons when I realize all that we have at our disposal and how much more we can do now in a lot less time.

If you need groceries but have three children under the age of five and have no one to watch them, that's okay. No need to bring them along for a shopping trip where, instead of buying groceries and getting out, you're running after them and putting the items back on the shelves that they've taken off! You can simply order those groceries online and have them delivered right to your doorstep.

How about when you borrowed forty dollars from your friend the other night and sent them the money without having to see them, with a note of thanks attached, through your phone using the Venmo app?

Remember the days when you could only get a cab in New York City by flailing your arms in the air with sheer panic and had to stand ready to body check anyone who tried to jump in the cab before you? Thanks to Uber and Lyft, you can calmly order a car from either app and track moment to moment where that car is. No more body checking necessary.

On the subject of driving, is anyone else out there directionally challenged? If so, dare we recall the days before GPS? The thought of having to use a regular map makes my head spin, so every time I get inside my car, I thank my lucky stars for this heavenly creation. (Except when it guides me the wrong way. Then I scream a lot of profanities.)

Sure, these may all seem like no big deal today because we've become used to the ease, but think about the time when these perks were not around. I sure as heck don't miss the days before Amazon Prime. Do you?

"Gratitude is one of the strongest and most transformative states of being. It shifts your perspective from lack to abundance and allows you to focus on the good in your life, which in turn pulls more goodness into your reality."
— Jen Sincero

The feeling of gratitude is one of the highest-level energy states, so when we're in that feeling, the laws of the Universe cannot help but bring us more things to be grateful for. I have started a habit of spending about ten minutes in gratitude as soon as I finish my morning meditation. I walk my dog, and I list all the things that I am grateful for—including my computer, phone, Bluetooth, and every device I use because they are tools that aid me in every aspect of my life. We have all become so accustomed to new school technology that most of the time, we take the marvel of digital technology for granted.

We need to take a second to remember that these advances are gifts, and they need to be appreciated too. We have so much more opportunity than our parents and grandparents could have ever dreamed of because of modern technology—remembering that makes the little frustrations not so frustrating.

Let's take some time to give attention to the ways new school technology helps improve our communication.

1. **We Are Virtually Connected.**
    Sometimes I sit here in total awe of how connected we are able to be through technology. Gone are the days, when you lived in a

different state, or country than your family, and couldn't see them until a physical trip was booked. Now we have an array of conduits to keep us seeing each other, even when we are far apart.

Geography may physically separate us,
but digital technology virtually unites us.

Besides keeping us connected to those we know and love, digital technology also opens the doors for us to globally interact with people we may never have had the chance to meet otherwise. When we're online, we can bond with people around the world and find common ground through the sharing of our dreams and struggles. Whether it's through "likes," and words of empowerment when we post about a win, or messages of encouragement and understanding when we post about hard times, we have a place to go to for love and support, which allows us to realize something beautiful:

We are all on the same team of humanity.

Sometimes we only focus on our differences as humans, but through the virtual world, we can begin to understand that we are all more alike than we think. When someone shares what they're going through, and it's something that we've also gone through, a similarity is recognized, and we realize we are not alone. Knowing you are not alone may be one of the most comforting realizations to the human spirit. The virtual world opens our eyes to the fact that no matter where we are in the world, we are all human beings complete with thoughts, feelings, and up and downs, and that automatically connects us.

Consequently, by understanding this fact, we become more aware of our judgments and begin to impede them. This understanding can then help us to develop more compassion, empathy, and kindness for the differences in our personal and professional relationships. Talk about a positive chain reaction, huh?

Reflections Section: *We Are Virtually Connected*

- How has digital technology kept you more connected to your loved ones?

_____

_____

_____

_____

- Write down a new person or group of people whom technology has connected you with.

_____

_____

- Reminisce and write about a time when you felt comforted by someone's encouragement online.

_____

_____

_____

_____

2. **Our Business Reach Is Extended.**
   In business, we no longer have to meet in person to create a connection with potential clients, consumers, or business partners because everything can be done online. With the power of video

calls and virtual meetings through Zoom, Skype, and other applications, we are able to create personal connections from behind a screen. Through online videos and video ads, we're able to emotionally reach people by introducing them to who we are and what we do, providing the possibility of gaining new business relationships. This is beyond incredible! Business.com found:

> Video content can spread brand awareness and build your business's community by establishing a connection between your company and its audience. According to a study from WowMakers, video on a landing page can increase conversion by at least 80%. Additionally, 40% of consumers believe video increases their likelihood of purchasing a product on their mobile device, with 76% of marketers claiming video produces more conversions than any other type of content.[7]

My coaching business is done primarily online, and I cannot tell you how thankful I am for the technology to be able to do this. The connections I have developed with my clients, who are from a variety of countries, would not have been possible if it weren't for the virtual world. A while back, when I was taking "The Knowledge Broker Blueprint" online course, I joined an accountability group, who would meet every Wednesday afternoon to talk through our progress, confusion, wins, and the tasks that we held each other accountable for. That group has turned into a beautiful bunch of friends who now share our business life fiascos and victories *and* our personal life fiascos and victories. On one of our calls last year, we decided it was time to take action and use what we had learned through the course and our

---

accountability group by creating something together. So, ten of us from seven different countries worked together—virtually—to create a five-day free challenge to help people go from stuck to unstoppable, and we called it the "Becoming Challenge." The event was a huge success, with more than one hundred people signed up who all learned new tools each day from the ten of us. When we completed the challenge, our group had a celebration call, and we all felt such pride for setting a goal for ourselves and reaching it, which could have only happened through the magic of technology. We still meet every week, and constantly laugh at the irony of how we feel so close, yet none of us have ever met in person!

If you're an author, think about the reach that you gain, by being able to sell your books online, as well as on Kindle, and audiobooks? You create new business relationships with each person who reads your words, instead of having to wait until they can get the book in bookstores.

No matter what business you may be in, technology provides you with more opportunity than ever before to extend your business reach and increase business relationships.

Reflections Section: *Our Business Reach Is Extended*

- How has technology improved your business?

_____

_____

_____

_____

- If you're not a business owner, how has technology made connecting with your favorite businesses more effortless?

_____

_____

_____

_____

3. **We Have Information at Our Fingertips.**

When you really take a second to think about how you can find information on just about any topic you can imagine, doesn't that blow your mind? I think about being in middle school and having to go to an actual library to leaf through books, and encyclopedias to find the information I needed. Truth be told, my best friend Jen and I loved the smell of the books, so we would happily inhale the scent of the pages as we searched for what we needed. Still, that took way longer than it does to search in a link bar!

We are exceptionally lucky to have limitless information and knowledge waiting there to be acquired whenever we're ready for it. Think about this: What if you started interacting with someone you're really interested in, but your first language is their second one, so there is a slight communication barrier? With the internet's speed and capabilities, you can download an application like Duolingo and learn some words and phrases from their native language to improve communication by your next conversation. This gesture will make them smile by showing them how much you care, strengthening the bond you're already creating. Now, does that make you feel grateful or what?

Reflections Section: *We Have Information at Our Fingertips*

- Record a few specific examples of things you accomplished through the internet that maybe you have taken for granted. (This could be something like getting in touch with someone you never thought you could until finding their contact info online.)

_____

_____

_____

4. **We Can Help Those in Need With Ease.**

The number of people in need in this world is astronomically high, and through the World Wide Web, we can be more aware of this. According to ActionAgainstHunger.org, "About 690 million people worldwide go to bed hungry each night.... An estimated 14 million children under the age of five worldwide suffer from severe acute malnutrition, also known as severe wasting, yet only 25 percent of severely malnourished children have access to lifesaving treatment."[8] With countless websites full of information like this, and the click of a button to donate, we can quickly and easily provide support. We have a better understanding of what is happening on this Earth, beyond updates that we receive here and there through snail mail or a commercial on television. When natural disasters, a missing person, or anything else significant happens that needs our attention, we have a greater capacity to be of service to our fellow teammates of humanity. By writing or sharing a post or starting a GoFundMe page, we spread awareness of the problem, offering a greater chance of a solution.

_____

8 https://www.actionagainsthunger.org/world-hunger-facts-statistics#:~:text=Around%20the%20world%2C%20more%20than,million%20people%20still%20go%20hungry.

"They say 'to serve is to love,' and I think to serve is to heal too."
— Viola Davis

Reflections Section: *We Can Help Those in Need with Ease*

- How have you been able to be of service thanks to technology?

_____

_____

_____

_____

- How has someone been of service to you or someone you know thanks to technology?

_____

_____

_____

_____

5. **We Can Be on Top of Our Health.**

   The most important relationship you have is with yourself. (I will continue to emphasize this point throughout our journey.) With that said, keeping up on your health is a major part of that relationship. Our health is precious, so anything that gives us a better chance of keeping it intact is an absolute advantage. The same goes for our loved ones. We always want them to do their best in being as healthy and strong as they can, too. In the medical world, the use of tests like PET scans, CAT scans, and MRIs allows doctors to detect conditions that otherwise could not have been detected. Moreover, for my hypochondriac friends (which has included me from time to time, to be very honest), you know the mental torture associated with unanswered medical questions. Well, now you don't have to wait to ask your general practitioner. There are doctors online you can talk to right away, instead of driving yourself crazy with "what ifs"! Besides the medical machines that help us in a doctor's office or hospital, there are loads of smart devices we can wear and applications we can download to track things like our blood pressure, blood sugar, how many steps we've taken, and our water consumption. A 2017 study was performed to see if the messaging app WhatsApp improved communication efficiency for an orthopedic team. Here is what the study found:

> Our study was intradepartmental, with all participants finding the use of WhatsApp made communication easier and quicker. The registrars felt that they had more regular updates on their patients than before while the interns felt that they were more supported with their decision-making as a result. With potentially more than 7,600 minutes saved on communication, all team members noted they had more time to perform clinical duties and participate in academic activities.[9]

How incredible is that? Through a digital app, a medical team was more efficient with their time, felt supported, and had more frequent updates on their patients' statuses, thus taking better care of their patients.

Let's not forget this as well: Technology is a life-saver. Having a car device like OnStar, or a smartwatch or cellphone that gives you access to quickly seeking medical attention in an emergency situation can literally *save a life*. This factor, in itself, plants the seed for eternal gratitude.

---

9   Ellanti, P. et al. "The Use of WhatsApp Smartphone Messaging Improves Communication Efficiency Within an Orthopaedic Surgery Team." *Cureus*. 2017. 9(2):e1040. Published 2017 Feb 18. doi:10.7759/cureus.1040.

Reflections Section: *We Can Be on Top of Our Health*

- How has technology played a part in improving or maintaining your health?

_____

_____

_____

- How has technology played a part in saving the life of someone you know or know of?

_____

_____

_____

6. **We Can Be More Creative.**

   Thanks to programs like Garage Band, musicians who are strapped for cash can still hone their craft and communicate through their music, and the ever-popular YouTube and TikTok have provided people with virtual stages for their talents to shine. Without these outlets, individuals may not have had the resources to have their skills seen by millions of people all over the world.

   When I was an actress living in New York City, but there was an audition in Los Angeles, I was able to record my audition (thank you high tech microphone and camera) at home and send it to LA because of the power of the internet. Do you understand the money and time I saved by not having to book a flight across the country? I was able to be seen and heard through the video so the people from the casting department could get a clear sense of who I was and then decide if they wanted to see more of me in person at a later time. See, our creativity and how we share that creativity no longer has to depend on other individuals or outside companies to help us because we don't have the right tools or skills. With digital technology, we now can learn any skill we desire, and we have the tools to create with greatness. In the privacy of our own homes! Even the Jetsons didn't have these capabilities!

Reflections Section: *We Can Be More Creative*

- What have you been able to do creatively that has been made possible by digital technology?

_____

_____

_____

7. **We Can Be Superheroes.**

Do you ever have those days where you feel like you can do it all? You write and send out important emails, you order all of your kid's Christmas presents online, you get a workout in, and you track the calories burned as you sweat. Then, you go to 1800flowers.com to send your parents a flower arrangement for their anniversary. You do the laundry while Facetiming your friend on her birthday, you receive your grocery delivery, make dinner, and because you've checked off everything on your to-do list, you get to sit on the couch and stream your favorite movie on HBO Max with a loved one.

I love those days, and I'm sure you do to. What I know is that those days are feasible because we can leverage so many of our tasks to technology. Think about it. No one can actually do it *all*, if they were in fact doing it all by themselves. Let's use the above example. Most of the accomplishments were done through the help of technology. Sending emails, ordering gifts online, tracking calories burned, sending flowers, Facetiming, grocery delivery, and streaming a movie. We all deserve to be superheroes sometimes, and with technology as our side-kick, we can!

Reflections Section: *We Can Be Superheroes*

- Write down a time when you felt like a superhero, checking off everything on your to-do list.

_____

_____

_____

_____

- Write down how many of your to-dos were leveraged to technology.

_____

_____

_____

- What forms of technology and pieces of technology are you most thankful for and why? (Have a tech-love fest and jot down everything you can think of. Trust me, doing this will jog your memory about beautiful moments in your life that only could have happened through technology.)

_____

_____

_____

_____

Thanks to the continuous rise of digital technology, we have more channels than ever before to be who we want to be and achieve what we want to achieve. It helps to remind ourselves of this when we want to throw our computer against the wall because the webpage isn't responding and the little wheel just keeps spinning and spinning!

Trust me, my friend, when you acknowledge and honor your resources, they will serve you even better than before. Have you ever noticed that when you show sincere appreciation when someone performs an act of kindness for you, it makes them want to do more of those acts? Well, when we show some love to the things we unconsciously rely on throughout the day, we'll find that they miraculously start to work better too. It's not just humans who require love, ya know.

By uncovering how technology both inhibits and improves our communication, we can now begin more consciously choosing the times we will use this incredible gift.

We can also begin more consciously to center in on every way, big or small, that technology serves us. Woohoo! Now, let's talk all about relationships.

Chapter Three:

RELATIONSHIPS

"Communication to a relationship is like oxygen to life.
Without it…it dies."
— Tony Gaskins

My best friend Melissa and I are the kinds of friends who could not talk for months, but the second we talk again, it's as if no time has passed. You know those kinds of friends? They're really the greatest, aren't they? Mel (my nickname for her) and I are more like sisters, and we call each other out right away when we know something is wrong or one of us is not being their best. A few weeks ago, I woke up to a text from her saying, "Thanks a lot for picking up my phone call!" I called her right away and when she answered, she greeted me with a sarcastic tone saying, "Oh, look who decided to call me back, finally!"

Confused, I asked, "What are you talking about?"

Mel told me she called me *a lot* the night before and was getting sent to voicemail every time, so she texted me, which I also didn't respond to. I kept saying I had *no* calls or texts from her that night (which was the truth,) so we began arguing. In the midst of the argument, I checked my phone and there were her missed calls. I apologized right away when I realized my phone had been on airplane mode, so I could write. I didn't turn off the airplane mode until that morning, which was when Mel's text came in from the previous night. In true Renée and Melissa fashion, once that was cleared up, we immediately moved on unscathed, but this got me thinking: How often has a close relationship of yours been strained because of a mis-communication through an electronic device?

Relationships make up our lives, and we can make or break a relation-ship based on how well we communicate. Even if you are the most intro-verted person, you still relate to others all the time. The customer service agent on the phone, your neighbor, your caretaker, a family member, a coworker, a friend, a significant other, and yes, even your pet. With each of these relationships, we must first give in the way we hope to receive, and we can do that by transparently communicating.

> *Taking the time to improve your communication skills*
> *will only serve you in every relationship, no matter*
> *how deep or casual the relationship may be.*

Today, we use texts and email quite often because of their convenience. They are great communication resources, but when they become the *only* resource, problems arise. Text and email messages, being devoid of voice inflection and body language, can often be unclear, and in our fast-paced society, that can make us easily jump to conclusions. The most straightfor-ward way to connect is in person, followed by video calls and phone calls. As I break down why, you may be thinking, *"Duh, this is obvious,"* but just because things are obvious doesn't mean we are always consciously aware of them. With that said, let's keep our minds open as we get a little bit technical here.

Let's start with a regular phone call. When you're on a regular phone call, the communication is much more clear-cut than through a text or email because you can hear the tone of someone's voice and the sound of their breath, as well as the silence. These give you pretty strong clues as to what that person is feeling. In *Alone Together*, Sherry Turkle talks about the difference between face-to-face and telephone compared to text and email, and writes: "But like the face-to-face interactions for which it substitutes, the telephone can deliver in ways that texts and emails cannot. All parties are present. If there are questions, they can be answered. People can express mixed feelings."[10]

When you're on a video call, communication is even more clear-cut because of the obvious addition of seeing facial expressions and body language. Both can tell us way more about what someone is feeling than just words.

Face-to-face offers the best understanding because you can hear what someone is saying, pick up on the tone they are using, observe their facial expressions and body language, and physically *feel* their energy.

The invisible power of our energy fields can speak volumes.

In all three of these communication channels, understanding goes both ways. The person you're talking to also receives the clues to how you're feeling.

In an email or text message, you can only see words, and since we all interpret words differently, what we mean may not be what the other person reads. To reference *Alone Together* once again, "In contrast, e-mail tends to go back and forth without resolution. Misunderstandings are frequent. Feelings get hurt. And the greater the misunderstanding, the greater the number of emails, far more than necessary."[11] Just the other day, my cousin Erica was texting me as I was on my way back from the airport. She asked, "Hey, how was your trip? It looked amazing." I saw the text right before I got out of the car, so quickly wrote, "Good."

---

10   Turkle, Sherry. *Alone Together: Why We Expect More From Technology and Less From Each Other.* New York: Basic Books, 2011. p. 167.
11   Ibid.

When I got inside, I unpacked, did laundry, got something to eat, and hours later, looked at my phone and realized Erica had texted me a few times asking first if I was okay. Then she asked, "Are you upset with me? I feel like you're giving me the cold shoulder." I picked up the phone to call her, opening with, "I am so sorry. I was texting you in the midst of my chaos and didn't go back to look until now." She understood, but admitted she had been convinced that something was off with me because my "good" response was abrupt. Since I hadn't responded to her other messages (shame on me), she felt upset because she thought I was mad at her. Take it from me, a thoughtless text or email message can be a recipe for disaster.

How many times has a friend used sarcasm over a text and caused you automatically to get defensive? Then, when you asked them about it in a slightly annoyed tone, they responded with something like, "Hey, relax. I was just playing around." Trust me, I understand that not every conversation can be in person or on the phone, but when a relationship is important, you want to have the best possible platform to articulate yourself.

Relationship with Self

> *"It takes courage to endure the sharp pains of self-discovery, rather than choose to take the dull pain of unconsciousness that would last the rest of our lives."*
> — Marianne Williamson

When I heard Jamie Kern Lima, the co-founder and CEO of IT Cosmetics, speak live at an event, I was blown away by her journey, but even more so by her genuine and grounded nature. I took copious notes to try and capture her nuggets of wisdom. Looking back at everything she said, I realize her success was activated by her strong relationship with *self*. Every time life presented her with a new obstacle or opportunity, Lima first listened to her gut. Here's a secret, my friend:

*You can only hear what your gut is saying
by being in constant communication with yourself.*

If you aren't staying in communication with yourself, you won't recognize when your instincts are trying to tell you something. Lima was a television news anchor, and when she was live on air, she heard her producer in her earpiece telling her something was on her face. That something was her hereditary rosacea showing through her makeup. Lima struggled to find makeup that covered her skin condition, and she realized if she was struggling, others were struggling too. With an innate desire to do great things by helping others, Lima understood that if she could solve this problem for herself, she could also solve it for others, and thus, her entrepreneurial quest to create a beauty product that worked began.

Lima started IT Cosmetics with her husband, Paulo, in their living room. Despite years of rejections, hurtful comments from potential investors, a diminishing bank account, and many nights crying herself to sleep, she kept going.

Through all of the hard times, Lima took the risks and stayed true to herself every step of the journey because authenticity as a person and authenticity as a company is key for her. On her first live QVC segment, Lima wiped off her makeup so viewers could see how the makeup was effective at covering up her rosacea. This decision went against what experts advised her, but she knew in her gut that the best way to serve her potential customers was to reveal her real self. The decision proved to be the right one because the "Sold Out" sign went up within minutes, and IT Cosmetics went on to become the largest luxury makeup brand in the country. Lima's authenticity shines through so brightly because by constantly listening to her gut through strong intrapersonal communication, she's discovered what *is* authentic to her personally and professionally. Jamie Kern Lima sold IT Cosmetics to L'Oréal for 1.2 billion dollars and became the first female CEO of a brand in L'Oréal's history! This is what's possible when you nurture your relationship with self, first and foremost!

If you don't have a strong relationship with self, how can you know who you are, what you want, and what you stand for?

In the spirit of Jamie Kern Lima, let's get real here, okay? We all have insecurities and unhealed wounds that subconsciously drive our actions. When we choose to ignore these layers of our being to avoid feeling pain, we cause more pain. The pain is the result of moving farther and farther away from who we truly are.

On the flip side, when we face our insecurities and wounds head on, when we *communicate* with ourselves through questions and giving ourselves the permission to feel whatever comes up, we move closer and closer to who we truly are. These questions can be as simple as, "How am I feeling today?" or "What is really bothering me?" or "How can I find a better way?"

Most of us have accumulated many subconscious habits throughout our lives, and these habits determine our actions in subtle ways we don't even realize.

When habits happen subconsciously, they become patterns, and patterns become difficult to break unless we challenge them by asking questions.

When you are honest and brave enough to start a dialogue regardless of the tears, anger, confusion, laughter, or fear, you take hold of the shadows that drove you, and reconnect to *you.*

Bonus: When you get really good at being in constant communication with yourself, you will get really good at communicating with others because your newly discovered self-awareness lowers your tolerance for any superficial interactions with the significant people in your life.

Asking questions and writing down the answers is an easy, yet valuable technique to enhance intrapersonal communication. The simple act of asking counteracts the avoidance pattern and lets you take the reins of your behavior.

Just as negative habits can turn into patterns, the same is true for positive ones. We've all started a habit, like washing our face each night or making our bed in the morning, that led to a pattern of doing that activity every day. Recognizing the positive patterns we already have confirms that we have the power to create a new positive pattern of openly and honestly communicating intrapersonally. Take some time to think about your negative and positive habits that turned into patterns; then answer the questions below while this information is fresh in your mind. Remember, continue to answer these questions as earnestly as you can because doing so will create a habit, and that habit will create a pattern of positive change.

Reflections Section: *Relationship With Self*

- What three questions will you commit to asking yourself and writing down answers to on a daily basis? (Example: "How am I feeling," "What is really bothering me," and "How can I make this better?") Once you write these down, write them in your journal, and/or on a Post-it to remind yourself to be in constant communication with yourself!

_____

_____

_____

_____

- Which of your habits have turned into negative patterns?

_____

_____

_____

• Which of your habits have turned into positive patterns?

_____

_____

_____

_____

Three Act Play

Have you ever created a whole story in your head about what someone "meant" when they said, emailed, or texted you a remark you didn't like and then reacted as if the intent you created was their actual intent? Meanwhile, you didn't really know the intent because you didn't ask, so you just went on building a story with made-up details and possible scenarios for why they said what they did? I call this the "Three Act Play." Like a play that has three acts, it is a long and drawn-out journey full of unnecessary drama because the main character—you—has not found the courage to stand up to the antagonist—the fear of asking—and until the main character does, they keep getting faced with more drama.

Now, this may work for the entertainment purposes of a play, but when it happens in real life, it's not as entertaining, am I right?

For example, my friend Pat and I were just talking about a guy she recently started dating. Everything was going super-well after two dates, and he had made it clear he wanted to see her again, but Pat was going out of town for a few months for work. The guy said he was cool with that and still wanted to stay in contact, but when Pat hadn't heard from him after the first few days of being away, the Three Act Play began.

Act One: Pat began ruminating on every possible reason he hadn't called. "I misread all of the signs." "He's dating someone else." "We didn't get intimate, so he lost interest."

Act Two: Then came the anger. "Forget him. I didn't really like him anyway." "Who does he think he is?" "If he tries to call, I won't even pick up the phone now."

Act Three: Last came the self-ego boost. "I'm too good for him anyway." "Wait until he sees me one day looking the best I ever have as I walk right past him." "I'm so much better off knowing he's not worth it now before I get in too deep."

Now, every Three Act Play is different in the emotions, and thoughts it conjures, but they are the same in that they all begin from a place of uncertainty.

As a friend, at this point, all you can really do is try to be the logical one, right? Well, that's when I said, "Why don't you just give him a call and ask how he is? Then if he acts standoffish, you move on with your life, feeling validated in everything you already decided about him."

She heeded my advice, gave him a call, and found she had been utterly mistaken. Her ruminations could not have been more wrong. The only reason he didn't call was that he'd been traveling too and wanted to give her some time to settle in before he reached out. Now, they are happily dating and planning their first vacation together.

This is the Three Act Play, my friend.

Pat wasted hours stressing herself out by not having an actual conversation with the guy. By asking the question you need answered or simply reaching out, you save time, energy, and a lot of emotional turmoil from assuming the truth of the situation. Again, I remind you, all this assuming really does is just make asses of you and me, so let's try to stop it, okay?

Full disclosure: I, myself, have gone into the Three Act Play over what an emoji meant in a text I received. Talk about hitting rock bottom.

The next time your day grinds to a halt because you get caught in the Three Act Play loop, please use the following affirmation:

When my brain starts spinning like a ball,
I must stop and give them a call!

That's right; a little rhyme never hurt anybody. This silly little phrase will interrupt the Three Act Play, closing it before it even opens, and push you to take action.

Reflections Section: *Three Act Play*

- Have you ever gone through the Three Act Play? If so, what was the situation? How did going through that mental trap feel?

_____

_____

_____

_____

- Have you ever watched someone else go through the Three Act Play? If so, what did you observe about that person while they went through it?

_____

_____

_____

_____

_____

Romantic Relationships

"Good communication is as stimulating as black coffee,
and just as hard to sleep after."
— Anne Morrow Lindbergh

About a month into dating my husband Michael, was my thirtieth birthday. All I wanted was a small dinner gathering with my closest friends and him. To me, having Michael there—sitting beside me at my birthday dinner—was *obviously* a sign of how I felt about him. I probably mentioned how special the day was to Michael only about fifty times, and I explained that my nearest and dearest would be there. This meant he would be meeting those special people for the first time, and we all know what a big deal that can be, right?

Well, the night was really great, but in the back of my mind, I was waiting for confirmation about how he felt about me, about us. I mean, I could tell he liked me after a month of exciting dates, and we had great chemistry, but we hadn't talked about where the relationship was going, so I had no concrete evidence. All I had were signs *hinting* at mutual feelings—but that wasn't enough for me.

The birthday dinner was on a Saturday, and my real birthday was the following Tuesday. I was performing in *Chaplin* on Broadway at the time, and that Tuesday of my birthday we had a performance. After the show, the cast and I went to celebrate my big day at one of our go-to spots in Midtown, Manhattan, and Michael joined us. After, he and I went back to my apartment, and as we were sitting on my couch, I decided that if he didn't step up and tell me how he felt, it would be our last date. (Why waste time, ya know?)

Well, after a little while, he must have sensed my energy because out of nowhere he said, "So, where is this going?" To which I said, "Well, why don't you tell me? I think I've made it very clear how I feel. You were the one beside me at my birthday dinner, and I've introduced you to everyone important in my life." His response, which we still laugh about to this day was, "Well, I have a really great time with you."

At this point, my internal monologue was, "If you can't do better than that, then I am *d-o-n-e*." My response back was where Renée's sassiness emerged with, "Well, I have a great time with the strangers I meet at Starbucks in the morning, so what does that mean?"

My comment must have lit a fire under him because he said, "You know how I feel about you. I like you so much, and I think we should do this." Well it's *about darn time*, Captain Obvious! That's all I needed. That little statement that made everything clear.

Looking back at the situation, I can see the irony. I did the *exact* same thing I judged Mike for. I gave "signs" that I really liked him, but I didn't actually *say* anything.

Side note: This is a great lesson. When you find yourself judging someone, take a moment to look within and be honest about whether you do the same thing that you're judging them for. Most of the time, the answer is yes because the things that trigger us in others are usually the parts of ourselves we dislike. This is great to understand because awareness is the first step in accepting and transforming those disliked parts within ourselves.

> *"Witnessing your judgement is an act of self-love*
> *and a major step toward healing."*
> — Gabrielle Bernstein

Once Michael actually told me how he felt, the communication floodgates were beautifully opened. Our conversation continued about our expectations for the relationship, and the first thing I told him was communication is most important to me. I explained that I believe talking and being open with each other is the foundation of a great relationship, and he could not agree more.

Wow! We both used our words, and what a difference it made. Five minutes earlier, I was picturing myself breaking it off with him, and then him begging for me back, to which I would sing, *"If ya liked it, then ya shoulda put a ring on it,"* and feeling all boss-babe like. Luckily, we simply found common ground through talking, so that didn't happen. I cannot explain what a relief it was once the floodgates of communication opened. It added another layer to my affinity for this man because he showed me he was just that—a man. He showed me he was not afraid to speak his mind and express his wants, needs, and expectations.

Here was the best part, though. He shared his vulnerability too, which I found most attractive. Michael admitted talking about his feelings and thoughts was not very familiar territory. He was used to keeping things to himself and working things out on his own. As the conversation progressed, he explained that since he now understood how important communication was to me, he would work on that and make it a priority. Bam. No more assuming or guessing necessary!

When you are clear about what you want, you cannot go wrong.

I realize being vulnerable can be scary. You may feel that openly sharing your expectations may scare the other person away and you'll be left alone and heartbroken. But let me ask you a question: Wouldn't you rather know that *now* than ten years down the road? If you can flip the script and realize that vulnerability is a key ingredient for strong relationships, then it won't feel as scary.

Here's the truth: We all have our "deal breakers" in relationships, which are the things we refuse to accept. I explained to Michael from the get-go exactly what my deal breaker was, which gave him a choice at that moment to accept or walk away. Even if he couldn't handle my need for strong communication and said, "Listen, that's not something I'm comfortable with, so I don't think this is going to work," that would have been okay, and here's why:

Clarity is power in all relationships.

Michael and I saved a lot of time and energy by talking sincerely and sharing our feelings and expectations. Having these talks will always start you off on the right foot because you're putting all your cards on the table.

When you do that, you give the other person a basic outline of what they're signing up for. Remember this, my friend:

> *It is always better to know upfront what someone's expectations are; then you can make an informed decision about whether you'd like to continue on with them.*

The more clarity we can provide and gain in return, the more power we possess—the power of knowing which direction we're going in. To this day, after being married for seven years, communication is still our most powerful tool. Even if one of us is having a tough day and we need a few minutes to ourselves before talking, we tell that to the other person. When we verbally express that, we don't waste time wondering and questioning if we caused the silence. Otherwise, it's like, "Oh, fine, babe; just because you're in a bad mood doesn't mean you have to ignore me!" Then the trail of unnecessary commotion begins, and for what? Because we couldn't just *say*, "Hey, I need a few minutes, and we'll talk about it later, okay?" How easy is that?

Well, I'll tell you this: It's much easier than it will be to argue for two hours about a bunch of assumptions. We've all been there, so let's work together to avoid the assuming and get right to the heart of the matter. Take the time now to write down an issue you've experienced in the love department based on a lack of verbal communication. Dig deep and ask yourself if a simple phone call or face-to-face conversation could have made a positive difference in the relationship. Digging deep is a major factor in making a change for the better to your habitual way of communicating.

Reflections Section: *Romantic Relationships*

- What is an issue you've experienced in the love department because of a lack of verbal communication? Be as specific as you can about the situation and the feelings that arose.

_____

_____

_____

_____

- Do you believe a phone call or face-to-face conversation could have either avoided the issue altogether or at least alleviated some of the tension? If so, how would things have been different?

_____

_____

_____

_____

Family/Friendships

> *"In life, the path of least resistance is always silence. If you don't express your feelings and thoughts to others, you don't have to deal with their reactions to it. You don't have to feel vulnerable. You don't risk rejection. But I'll tell you what: the path of least resistance leads exactly where that ride leads to…. Nowhere."*
> — Brendon Burchard

Family relationships can sometimes be the trickiest of all because we often hold things in and suppress our true feelings for the sake of keeping the peace. Keeping the peace is a beautiful goal, but by continually suppressing our real feelings, resentments form, and resentments can result in big blowups or estrangements.

One of my clients, Tracy, was dealing with a recurring family matter. Tracy grew up with her parents and her sister Natalie. From the time she was young, she felt a divide existed between her and her sister. As the only two girls in the family, Tracy wanted so badly to have a great relationship with her sister, but Natalie made it clear she didn't have any interest in being close.

Tracy, along with the rest of the family, recognized Natalie's cold ways and her tendency to make hurtful, passive-aggressive comments, but no one said a word. Tracy never wanted to cause a stir by saying something to her sister, so she talked to her mother about the problem, hoping, as the matriarch of the home, her mother could talk sense to Natalie. Her mother's response was always the same, "That's just Natalie." Tracy knew her mother just wanted to keep the peace, so Tracy followed suit. Therefore, Natalie was never confronted about her disrespectful and unkind comments, and as the years went on, her relationship with Tracy remained the same.

Today, the sisters each have their own children, and although Tracy and Natalie are not close, their children are tight-knit cousins. A couple of years ago, when the entire family came together for a family dinner, the unstated feelings could not be held in any longer. Tracy's three-year-old daughter was trying get Aunt Natalie's attention to have her come play with her. For five minutes, Tracy could feel the heat rising inside as she watched Natalie ignore her precious baby, and to add fuel to Tracy's fire, Natalie then called over her own daughter to say, "Can you just go play with her?"

The disgust and rage Tracy felt were enough to make her explode. The next thing she knew, she was screaming at Natalie, unleashing layers upon layers of hurt and anger that she had kept inside since childhood. The whole family started arguing, including Tracy's parents, who did everything they could to end the fight and move on, but nothing could stop the release of what had too long been buried.

Natalie, her husband, and their two children eventually walked out of the house, slamming the front door. Inside, Tracy's parents and her children stood in tears, while Tracy and her husband took conscious deep breaths to bring their blood pressure under control.

This story illustrates why, despite our tendency to avoid conflict, dealing with an issue right away, before that issue stacks, is a better choice.

Things swept under the rug never stay there forever. Eventually, they always creep back out all over your sparkling-clean hardwood floors.

When you handle an issue in its infancy, before it grows into an angry teenager, then an out-of-control young adult, and finally into a full-blown adult, you have more of a chance of keeping the peace you desire. You can avoid situations like Tracy's by making it your intention to speak from the heart when something begins to upset you, rather than waiting until you are already at your wits' end.

That said, there is no need to turn little annoyances into big ordeals, but if someone repeatedly says or does something that hurts you, then speak from the heart. By doing so, you will prevent needless turmoil and probably end up even closer to that person than you were before.

Sometimes, the problems you find yourself in with family or friends do not begin in person, where you have a better picture of what's going on, but instead, they begin as a text message. You send a text to a friend, and when the response is not what you expect, instead of picking up the phone to clarify, you text back from a place of assuming the intention of their text, and the problem is exacerbated.

To be completely honest, I really enjoy texting, but when it comes to serious, essential topics, I dial faster than you can text "Hi." The bottom line is that the real issues occur when we *just* text or email, so let's use those options as *a* tool and not *the* only tool, okay?

Recently, one of my closest friends was angry with me, but the only indication I had of this was a snarky text. I was completely caught off guard, so I immediately picked up the phone, thinking, *Why are you wasting time texting me when you can just call me?* She didn't answer the phone, sending me straight to voicemail. My insides churned with frustration!

I was distraught. Yes, I was upset because she was upset with me, but I was more upset because she was not communicating with me. Months of not speaking went by, and when she finally agreed to talk with me, Pandora's box opened. After some arguing and releasing feelings, we found the root of the problem to be a few small situations that were entirely misread, and never talked about. We wasted months not speaking and being unnecessarily aggravated due to *a simple lack of communication*!

Doesn't that seem like a big price to pay for skipping an honest conversation? We both lost energy and the most precious libation in this life—time. Here is a truth bomb, my friend, to keep with you as a reminder as you move through life.

Time is the only thing we cannot get back.

We can lose material things like money and real estate and gain them back, and we can even lose friendships and gain those back, but time cannot be regained once it is lost. Every moment spent ruminating rather than taking action results in a loss of the limited time we are given.

Speaking up is not natural for everyone, but here is where we can learn how to do it. When there is discord in a relationship and your fear tells you it's better to ignore it than speak up, without delay, ask yourself, "Is running away from the fear worth the loss of the one thing I cannot get back?"

Hopefully, your answer will be a big ol' "No." But if that is not enough to make you step up, then try the following.

Start by writing a letter (yes, with a pen and paper). It will allow you to organize your thoughts so you know what you need to say before you say it—then it won't be as terrifying. Next, you can either send the letter through regular mail, which can be the beginning of a deep conversation (or correspondence), or you can get right to facing the giant. After getting the thoughts down on paper, pick up the phone to have the conversation or set a time to meet in person and have the conversation, no matter how uncomfortable. One more truth bomb for you since we're on a roll here. Being uncomfortable happens to us all through experiences we *do not choose*. In that event, since we're going to have to get uncomfortable anyway…

***Let's get comfortable with being uncomfortable
by choosing to take action on what we're afraid of.***

I believe being uncomfortable for a brief period is way better than living with negative energy for a long period while you're just delaying the inevitable! Just rip that bandage of fear off (aka have the talk), and before you know it, the sting is all gone (aka the fuss has subsided, and you can get back to your regularly scheduled life).

Right now, in the Reflections Section below, please use a few moments to take inventory of the problems you've faced in your family or friendships because of miscommunication. Just like you did for romantic relationships, be as honest with yourself as you can in writing these problems down because they will serve you in finding better communication habits.

Reflections Section: *Family/Friendships*

- What are a couple of issues you've experienced with family and/or friends because of a lack of verbal communication? Be as specific as you can about the situations and the feelings that arose.

_____

_____

_____

_____

_____

- Do you believe a phone call or face-to-face conversation could have either avoided the issues altogether or at least alleviated some of the tension? If so, how would things have been different?

_____

_____

_____

_____

_____

Professional Relationships

> *"Technology does not run an enterprise, relationships do."*
> — Patricia Fripp

When I was researching how to get my book published and what that entailed, I came across a man who is extremely knowledgeable about writing and publishing. He was a former literary agent who now coaches authors. He provided some really helpful online resources and had an offering to go over the first fifty pages of your book during a one-on-one, hour-long call.

I learned so much from the resources he provided that I decided to take advantage of the offering. Once I signed up and paid him via the net, he sent me a detailed questionnaire with sixty questions I needed to answer and send back to him along with my fifty pages. Well, right after I sent him the money, some fear set in. *Renée, did you even research this guy? Fraud happens all the time, and you just sent money to someone you haven't even spoken to! Oh, my God*, I thought.

Nervously, I looked up his company's phone number and called. After one ring, an odd voice recording recited the name of the company and asked me to leave a message. I panicked, but I left a voicemail with my name asking him to please call me back.

One second later, I was emailing the address I found online—sending an email with the same panic I was feeling. I wrote, "Hello. I just called your phone number and a voice recording picked up right away, and I would like to make sure that everything here is legit, as I just sent you money and haven't spoken to you yet. I look forward to hearing back from you."

He responded later that day, explaining that the number was his and he had been on a call when I rang. I wrote back very honestly admitting that with all of the scams out there, you can't be too careful, and he agreed.

Three days later, I was happily filling out the in-depth questionnaire to send with my fifty pages, and a question popped in my head. I wondered if I was supposed to have anyone who reads my manuscript sign a non-disclosure agreement (NDA), so I emailed him the question and was totally taken aback by his response. He said he did not want to work with me at that point because he could tell I was more nervous than excited. He explained, between the first email exchange and the NDA question, he didn't think I trusted him and his credentials.

I was absolutely disappointed, first, because I was so excited about our session, and second, because it was a *complete* miscommunication. After feeling upset for a while, I took a few minutes to step outside of myself and understand exactly where he was coming from. Here we were communicating through email, where he could not tell my tone nor my intentions, so there was a lot of space for interpretation. Then I had a moment of clarity: This was the *perfect* lesson for me to be having at the *perfect* moment. I was in the midst of writing a book about preventing this exact kind of miscommunication, so, *of course*, I needed to go through this situation!

I emailed him back, apologizing wholeheartedly for offending him. I told him that when I asked him about the NDA, it was because the entire world of book writing was new to me, so I turned to him for his expertise in this area. He wrote back and thanked me for clearing up the confusion, and when we finally spoke, I told him, "The whole premise of my book is about communication and how it can often get misconstrued through email and texts. I may have to include this story in the book."

We laughed about it, and here we are. I get to use this real-life example to illustrate how our professional relationships can quickly go awry if we are not willing to go beyond texting and emailing in our communication. I am confident that if I picked up the phone to ask him the NDA question, the misunderstanding would not have happened because he would have heard my sincerity in asking his advice and my excitement about our upcoming call.

When we think of "professional" relationships, we often only consider the workplace, but we handle numerous "business" interactions outside of our jobs. What about your financial advisor, or doctor, or child's swim instructor, or child's teacher? These people are dealing with major aspects of your life—your money, your health, and your children—so it is crucial to have error-free communication with them. Tremendously crucial.

Throughout my life, I always thought I was the Queen Multitasker, juggling ten things at once and applauding myself for doing so until I realized I was dropping the ball and getting a little "messy" in my tasks.

When I showed up for my first appointment with my therapist (which I had to wait two months to get), the door was locked. As I stood in the rain, looking behind me at an empty parking lot, I knew something was off. I called the therapist's cell phone, and when he answered, I said, "Hi, Doc. I'm outside the front door of your office, but it's locked." He said, "Your appointment was yesterday. I'm not there on Thursdays."

Oh, no, I thought. *Great first impression, Renée; now you look like a flake. You* are *a flake!"* What I said was, "I am so sorry. I am looking at my calendar, and for some reason I wrote down today for our appointment. Is there any way I could be fit in next week?" He kindly gave me another appointment, probably dreading taking me on as a client, and I drove home feeling crappy about myself.

This was when I realized that being a good multitasker does not necessarily mean you are "good" at the tasks you're doing. In this situation, I was obviously wearing my multitasker crown proudly and not entirely listening to the doctor when we spoke on the phone. While we were setting up the appointment, I'm sure I was thinking about one of my many other tasks.

As we talked about in Chapter Two, *listening* is a major player in the game of communication, and these kinds of situations follow when we don't listen. We show up to a locked building in an empty parking lot in the rain and are disappointed in ourselves.

So, I decided to hang up my Queen Multitasker crown and begin refocusing my priorities. I'm happy to report that now when my therapist and I set up appointments, I take the time to immediately record the date and time. I also repeat the day and time back to him to be as clear as glass! Our business relationships, even though some have a short and specific timeline, require precise communication.

What information do you need to relay to the contractor who is renovating your kitchen? Let me tell you firsthand, if you are not 100 percent upfront and transparent in communicating what you expect, you will not get the dream kitchen from the photo you cut out of *Better Homes and Gardens* and posted on your vision board.

In every business, technology plays an intricate part. Whether you are an engineer, life coach, teacher, lawyer, author, salesperson, or musician, you use technology in some capacity to conduct business. In several vocations, computers are the main tool and, therefore, become the main source of communication among coworkers. The same is true for phones, which are now minicomputers, more powerful than the best personal computers available in the 1990s. Because of this, there is more likelihood for misunderstandings to occur with the addition of electronic error to human error.

An email may not send properly, writing in all caps may make someone think the sender is angry, a response may take longer than is comfortable, someone may not read an email in the way it was intended, or there is bad service in an area and a text with a solution to an important issue is never sent. These are all real challenges we face when we don't have time for verbal contact.

As the dance captain of *Pretty Woman: The Musical* on Broadway, a part of my job was to be there for the understudies if they wanted to run through any choreography with the actors they'd be dancing with before a performance. One day my boss and I were texting about rehearsing a lift before a show with two actors who had not performed the lift together in a while. When my boss checked in with both actors via text, they said they felt comfortable and didn't need to rehearse.

Onstage at showtime, I was with the actor who would be lifted and figured I'd remind her once more about the lift. Her face dropped, and she said, "What? I thought it was with a different person?" Well, my heart began beating out of my chest as I quickly and quietly explained what would be happening. Thank goodness everyone was safe, and the lift went fine, but afterward, we all spoke in person. She had simply misread the text, and because she had been lifted by someone else in the past, she assumed our boss was referring to him. (There is that dangerous word again—assume.) This moment confirmed what I instinctually knew to be true.

Even if some of our business can be done through our fingers, all of it cannot.

In the moment after receiving the information from my boss, the best thing for me to do would have been to take two minutes to verbally and individually check-in with the actors.

Verbally checking in takes out the room for mistakes to be made when you only communicate through texts or email. Now, in my current work as a communication coach, when I teach any course, I make sure to verbally state what those attending can expect from the course and what the course is not about. That way, everyone has all the information up front, and no gray area exists to cause miscommunication.

When it comes to being the leader of any company or team, it is important to see yourself as the *trendsetter*. If you want things to run as smoothly as possible (which is a smart goal for any leader), strong communication needs to be one of the trends that you set.

You're the example for those you are leading, so if they do not see you communicating clearly and candidly, you can anticipate that they will do the same.

In a study titled "The Impact of Using Technology-Based Communication on Quality of Work Relationships," researchers Madara Pratt and Sarma Cakula looked at leadership. "...authors recognize the importance of leadership as the most important role in maintaining good quality of relationships within the company. Leaders have more challenges within virtual teams than those who work mostly face-to-face."[12]

In regards to virtual teams, having to manage a team from different locations, through a screen, while each person has their own specific set of distractions, can present more challenges than when everyone is physically together in one place. Therefore, leading with distinct communication is even more imperative so that through your guidance, each person knows exactly what is required in their roles.

Everything flows from the top down.

Think about this: As a leader, if your team barely sees you around physically or virtually, and the only interaction you share with them is through email or a newsletter, what kind of company dynamic would you be building? You can bet that it will be much less team-like than if you visited the workplace or virtual place often to check-in, provided a forum for questions, and left them with some heartfelt gratitude for being a part of your team.

I have seen firsthand how businesses struggle when there are holes in communication and how beautifully companies run when everyone knows exactly what is expected of them and where to turn when they have a question. I, for one, like the latter much better.

---

12 Pratt, Madara and Sarma Cakula. "The Impact of Using Technology-Based Communication on Quality of Work Relationships." *Baltic J. Modern Computing.* 8.1 (2020): 143-153. https://doi.org/10.22364/bjmc.2020.8.1.07.

The study above also explored ways to improve workplace relationships concluding:

> First of all, the most important is to have face-to-face meetings in initial phase of employment. Also, it is suggested to have periodic face-to-face meetings afterwards. Company meetings and training programs are beneficial for developing better social relationships among members of the company. Employee-employee relationships are also important. These peer relationships create bonds and trust in the team and company.[13]

Relationships within the workplace are vital because tension between coworkers causes negative energy that can detrimentally affect everyone's ability to do their job effectively. On the other hand, an atmosphere of positivity and camaraderie, with open channels of communication starting from the top down, allows everyone involved to flourish and enjoy the workplace.

One of my favorite phrases to live by is, "Teamwork makes the dream work," by John C. Maxwell. When evident and direct communication is the standard in a business, everyone on that team can work as a unit, making the vision of that business come to fruition!

Reflections Section: *Professional Relationships*

- What is an issue you've experienced with a boss or coworker because of a lack of verbal communication? Be as specific as you can about the situation and the feelings that arose.

_____

_____

_____

_____

13   Ibid.

- Do you believe a phone call or face-to-face conversation could have either avoided the issue altogether or at least alleviated some of the tension? If so, how would things have been different?

_____

_____

_____

_____

- Can you recall a positive workplace/virtual place experience that stemmed from a boss who set a strong standard of communication within the company? Elaborate on this.

_____

_____

_____

_____

The more we nurture our relationships—intrapersonally, with family, friends, and professionally, through practicing transparent communication, the more confidence and clarity we obtain in those relationships.

In the next chapter, we will take it back to the days before digital technology was introduced and delve into what qualities from those days we can intersperse into our lives now to ground us and bring in more of that ol' school simplicity.

Chapter Four:

OL' SCHOOL SIMPLICITY (PRE-DIGITAL TECHNOLOGY)

*"Sometimes you have to disconnect to stay connected.
Remember the old days when you had eye contact during
a conversation? When everyone wasn't looking down at a device
in their hands? We've become so focused on that tiny screen that
we forget the big picture, the people right in front of us."*
— Regina Brett

A few years ago, I was talking with a wonderful woman who was at my friend's home when I went to visit him for Christmas. She was eighty-seven, born in 1932, and a former teacher. As we talked about the vast differences in life she had experienced over eight decades, I told her I was writing this book. She then told me this incredible story about how when she was a child, she would sit down with her mother, father, and six brothers and sisters for dinner. After dinner, her mother would push aside the table and her father would grab his violin. All of the kids would take turns doing the polka with her mother in the kitchen. Then, after a bit, her father would grab his flute (made with his own two hands out of copper tubing) and play as the kids continued to dance around in pure joy. As she spoke about the memory, her face lit up and she smiled as if she were right back in that kitchen. What a beautiful memory to have where every member of the family was engaged with one another without any outside distractions. How many precious memories can you recall when you were entirely present with those around you? When you felt fully engaged and fully alive in that moment? When you didn't have something pulling you away from the here and now?

Before we were all privy to televisions that could record our favorite shows, and the internet, and phones that make us capable of ruling the world, "times were simpler," as my grandparents would say. People worked only with their own minds and bodies for what they needed. Building physical strength did not happen at a gym, with machines that helped to isolate different muscle groups, but as a byproduct of daily tasks. For example, before washing machines were created, women used their hands, forearms, and backs to wring out the heavy water dripping from the clothing items before laying them out to dry. In *Technology and Women's Voices: Keeping in Touch*, author Leto shares, "Women would congregate at the head of the stream because they had to rely on the solvent power of the water to clean their clothes. After crouching several hours by the water to wash clothes, women spread the clean items over rocks or bushes to dry, and visited while they waited."[14]

When people took on new projects, they had to figure everything out on their own because before the internet existed, there were no such things as video tutorials to show people how to "DIY" (do it yourself). Pre-digital technology, when children wanted to play, they created games from physical items like rocks, ropes, and paper, and enjoyment arose from running around outside in the neighborhood and doing cartwheels and handstands on the front lawn. (Okay, maybe that one was just personal to me, but you get my drift.)

---

14 Kramarae, Cheris. "Technology and Women's Voices." 1988. Routledge, Chapman and Hall, New York. Reviewed in *Bulletin of Science, Technology & Society.* 10.3 (June 1990): 138. https://doi.org/10.1177/027046769001000318.

Consequently, the activities that were available were enjoyed fully. When a person went for a walk outside, they were without a gadget to keep them constantly accessible. Therefore, they could take in the scenery wholly, and be *in* nature, rather than simply *passing through* it to get to the next activity. As Gazzaley and Rosen bring up in *The Distracted Mind*:

> Most of us carry an accessibility portal in our pocket or purse at all times, including…close at hand while we sleep….Of note, the accessibility is not just our ease in reaching out to our technology to forage information. It is also the very powerful way in which *technology can now reach out to us*. This truly changes everything. It would be as if a neighboring tree could go ahead and throw a nut at a squirrel any time it was interested in being fed upon.[15]

If someone were bored, they could participate in activities that kept them entertained, like reading a book or riding their bike, playing cards, or board games. The difference between now and then is those activities had nothing to do with entering another world led by a computer. In *Psychology Today*, Jim Taylor states:

> Technology conditions the brain to pay attention to information very differently than reading. The metaphor that Nicholas Carr uses is the difference between scuba diving and jet skiing. Book reading is like scuba diving in which the diver is submerged in a quiet, visually restricted, slow-paced setting with few distractions and, as a result, is required to focus narrowly and think deeply on the limited information that is available to them. In contrast, using the Internet is like jet skiing, in which the jet skier is skimming along the surface of the water at high speed, exposed to a broad

---

15   Gazzaley, Adam and Larry D. Rosen. *The Distracted Mind: Ancient Brains in a High-Tech World.* Cambridge, MA: MIT Press, 2016.

vista, surrounded by many distractions, and only able to focus fleetingly on any one thing.[16]

Pre-digital technology, people couldn't just pick up their phone and play *Words with Friends* or watch a funny TikTok video. They couldn't just purchase something on Amazon.com to lift their spirits, but what could lift their spirits was taking part in basic back-and-forth conversations for the sake of conversing. Now, we have texting, emailing, virtual "waving," and dropping into someone's direct messages, so starting a conversation just for the simple purpose of connecting with another human being is rarer. Today, we have the capability to find out everything about a person, from where they live and who their exes are to the mistakes they made in childhood before we even physically say hello to them. When you really think about it, that takes away a part of the adventure of learning about someone. I don't know about you, but as cool as technology is, the profoundly ol' school part of my soul loves the surprise of not knowing everything about someone beforehand. I love that time in a relationship when, with each new discovery, you eagerly put together the puzzle pieces. The puzzle you will either invest more time into or walk away from, depending on what you discover. Side note: I also loved the time as a young girl when I could be silly and free with my friends, never thinking twice if someone had their phone out recording us! It freaks me out, you know? I digress, but as grateful as I am for all we have at our disposal nowadays, I do realize some of what we have is at the cost of our own privacy. This is where I can fully grasp the upside of the pre-digital technology days.

"Artificial intelligence is not human intelligence.
People are mindful; computers are mindless."
— Nicholas Carr

16　Taylor, Jim. "How Technology Is Changing the Way Children Think and Focus." *Psychology Today.* December 4, 2012. https://www.psychologytoday.com/us/blog/the-power-prime/201212/how-technology-is-changing-the-way-children-think-and-focus.

Speaking of the upside of pre-technology days, I am at the moment, writing this chapter as I sit in the heart of Florence, Italy, among the masterpieces created by some of the most prestigious artists in history. People like Michelangelo and Leonardo da Vinci didn't have complex machinery or computers to aid them in creating their art. They had their hands, their brains, and perhaps a chisel and a mallet. Can you even imagine? My husband and I stepped inside the Academia Museum yesterday, and as we turned the corner from the entrance, we were literally stopped in our tracks. There, straight down the hallway, stood the most extraordinary statue—Michelangelo's *David*. It took our breaths away. The statue took Michelangelo over two years to complete, and it stands perfectly tall today as if it were made yesterday. Crowds gathered around the piece in awe of the details that make this sculpture so lifelike. From the veins in *David's* hand to the definition in each of his ribs, one cannot help but think, "How? How did *one* person build this?" With one slab of marble, a timeless tour de force was brought into existence, and people travel from all over the world to experience its magic. As my husband and I sat on a bench in the museum staring at the wonder that is *David*, I felt a sense of immense pride wash over me.

I was happily reminded of what we humans are capable of when not bombarded with distractions to take us off our path.

Could you envision how effective Michelangelo would have been if, while working on *David*, he had his cellphone in his back pocket vibrating every twenty minutes, with people calling him for other jobs? What about if he had his laptop open and the sounds of notifications were going off while he worked to concentrate on sculpting the statue's strong right leg or the intricacies of its fingers? Listen; I'm sure he would make it work, but I do not believe the sculpture would be half as amazing if he had all of the added interruptions that we have today. This is not to say that people who lived prior to pre-digital technology didn't have their share of worries and obstacles that could divert their attention, because of course they did. I am saying that the attention-stealers through sensory-overload that exists from digital technology are not something that stood in the way of their creative flow.

As Michelangelo was working, he didn't have the option of hopping on Facebook to check out what his competition was working on and wasting energy by going into comparison mode. He also didn't have the instruments to film his process of sculpting the marble into a stroke of genius so he could post on YouTube later. When he completed the masterpiece, he didn't need to spend time composing the perfect Instagram post, with the right number of hashtags, to promote his most recent work. This all exemplifies that his awareness never had to move to a virtual world, thus giving him more time for intentional focus on the real world in front of him, and what that meant for his creation.

Pre-digital technology, when people worked on more than one project at a time, like a writer, working on a couple of manuscripts, there were not multi-media sources to change their focus, from a physical action like writing to screen-based stimulation like the television or internet. Jim Kwik points out in his book, *Limitless*: "Compared to the 15th century, we now consume as much data in a single day as an average person from the 1400s would have absorbed in an entire lifetime."[17]

With all of the various streams of handling tasks and receiving information today, our ability to focus on one singular task or project has become more difficult because when we're on one information medium, another appears. You're on Pinterest following a recipe for shrimp to make for dinner when an email notification shows up, driving you to your inbox. The email is one you've been waiting for from your accountant, and it's about paperwork that needs to be filled out asap. You figure you can leave the shrimp simmering for a few minutes as you print the paperwork, and respond to a few texts you've been meaning to answer. Before you even

---

17 Kwik, Jim. *Limitless: Upgrade Your Brain, Learn Anything Faster, and Unlock Your Exceptional Life.* Carlsbad, CA: Hay House, 2020.

realize it, twenty minutes have gone by, the shrimp is overcooked—too rubbery even to chew, and you still haven't sent back the paperwork because you got sidetracked with giving your friend text advice.

Multitasking more often than not leads to a lack of attention to detail, and while we can multitask, is it serving us? Do we want to be the Jack of all trades, but the master of none?

A 2009 study on multitasking, called "Cognitive Control in Media Multitaskers," showed that "heavy media multitaskers are distracted by the multiple streams of media they are consuming, or, alternatively, that those who infrequently multitask are more effective at volitionally allocating their attention in the face of distractions."[18]

Let's be really candid here, my friend:

How fruitful can we actually be when we're taking on ten projects at once but giving our undivided attention to none?

Thank goodness Michelangelo didn't have the overload of digital distractions that are present today when working on *David* because what makes the statue so outstanding *is* the attention to detail. Even after seeing its magnificence in person, I still find it hard to grasp the reality that it was the job of one single person. One mind. One set of hands. One immense will to keep going. I just looked at more photos of the seventeen-foot pillar of tenacity as if my dissecting every part of it would help me better understand. I mean, *David's* complex expression represents such layered feelings that it appears like he could unfreeze from his position at any moment and move about the world right now.

We are all incredibly lucky to have endless resources like the internet at our fingertips, but it's important to remember that this was not always the case and still is not for so many. Honoring those who came before us and

---

18   Ophir, Eyal et al. "Cognitive Control in Media Multitaskers." Proceedings of the National Academy of Sciences of the United States of America. 106.37 (2009): 15583-7. doi:10.1073/pnas.0903620106.

recognizing what they achieved without all the bells and whistles we have today can remind us that everything we need is within us, and not outside of us. In turn, we can use technology as the gift it is, and not as a crutch. When you see the intricate craftsmanship and specifics of a piece as profound as *David*, you cannot help but feel inspired by those "simpler times" and yearn to find more of those simple moments in your own life.

The coolest part of all is that Michelangelo was a human and, therefore, made of the same stuff we are, so we share the same possibilities. Did you hear that? We are capable of doing what Michelangelo did. Yup, I said it!

> *Our potential is limitless. The only way it is not activated*
> *is through our lack of belief in this truth.*

Spending time in Florence is such an awakening to how incredible true presence feels. The urgency I am used to experiencing in my daily life is missing, making me wonder why. Yes, being on vacation always brings with it a lack of urgency, but there is something else. In asking myself this question, I attribute the difference to the surroundings. Everywhere you turn in Florence, you're right next to exquisite architecture or Renaissance art, so you cannot help but slow down and take in the beauty. The picturesque, historical atmosphere envelops you, subconsciously teaching you what it means to sit back, slow down, and focus on the here and now. My aunt and uncle, who frequently travel to Italy, learned an Italian belief from their tour guide: "If you don't have the time to stop and have a cup of coffee, life's not worth living!" In fact, in many regions of the country, coffee shops do not even have to-go cups to accommodate you dashing off with your *caffè*. Just seeing how the native Italians leisurely enjoy their meals and their conversations is refreshing. They exude ease while eating and drinking, which is often accompanied by laughter and then dessert. Eating is always at the top of my favorite activities list, and in Italy, the meals are extra-special. Each one feels like an experience within itself, as opposed to only being the delicious transition between activities. Every time I take a bite, I can taste each flavor, and when I sip the wine, I discover new adjectives to describe the taste profile.

Rick Steves puts it beautifully in his Italy guidebook: "If America's specialty is fast food, Italy's is slow food—bought daily, prepared with love and enjoyed convivially. Three-hour restaurant meals are common; dinner is the evening's entertainment. To 'eat and run' is seen as a lost opportunity."[19] Boy, is he right! There are no servers taking away your plate before you've finished chewing or dropping the bill before you've seen dessert. Quite the contrary. Sometimes, you wonder if they've decided to go home before even giving you the bill. I am *a-okay* with that. The pure act of sitting down with no other reason than being there, in that moment, is incredible. I can feel my body thanking me for falling into the calm energy. Michael and I, who are both type-A personalities, feel as if a weight has been removed from our shoulders—and that weight is called rushing.

Although there are many pros to being type-A, one con is rushing to get this and that accomplished because it can be exhausting. It's like a constant race with yourself, leaving those around you wondering why the heck you're moving so fast.

In Italy, the need to rush melts away completely and time slows down. The days feel as if some enchanted fairy has waved a mystical wand and added extra time to the calendar.

In addition to the culture itself, I realize that much of the absence of the rapid pulse is due to the lack of attachment to my cellphone. Usually when I've been on my phone nonstop going from one application to the next, at the end of the day, I find myself asking, "Where did the day go?"

***It feels like technology use causes the Universe
to press the fast-forward button on our lives.***

---

19   Steves, Rick. *Rick Steves Italy 2018.* New York: Avalon Travel Publishing, 2017. p. 6.

Here, when we get back to our place each night, I feel like we had a completely full day that felt more like three days than one. Spending time in Italy without using my electronic gadgets like they're an extra limb makes me feel like what I can only imagine people felt like before the electronic communications era. Free from the need to be ever-accessible. I'm barely using my phone except to take photos, and I'm only using my computer to write this chapter in real-time as I'm experiencing these moments. Otherwise, my focus is on what I am witnessing in front of me—Michael, the architecture, the food, the animals, the shops, the smell of real leather, the gelato!

With all the alerts, alarms, and notifications that come with new school technology, it's a real win when we can keep our focus on any *one* thing for any length of time. When I make the decision to dedicate time to *just* writing, do you know the mental discipline required to succeed? I must clear my calendar, make sure my family is good and I am not essential to their schedule, find a place where I will have absolutely no interruptions, light the candles, burn the sage, close out every tab on my computer, choose to ignore all the emails, put the to-do list out of my head for another day, put the phone on airplane mode, then put the phone face down so I don't get tempted when I see it light up, and make space for the creativity to flow through me.

This is *no joke*. Once I finally sit down, I need to decompress for a few minutes before I even touch the keyboard.

Usually, my ideal place to write is beside a beach or in some other exquisite part of nature, because in nature, the only sounds I hear are those that contribute to my focus, not take away from it. Replacing the unnatural sound of a Bluetooth speaker is the calming sound of the waves visiting the shore. In place of a Cheetos ad automatically playing online are the seagulls revving up to enjoy someone's dropped Cheetos. Instead of a smart TV subliminally working to control my beliefs is the sweet wind making its presence known.

If I don't have the chance to be somewhere besides my home to write, I like to write before 7 a.m. when it feels as if the world is quiet, and the hustle and bustle of the morning and midday hours has not begun. I am not yet battling with everyday responsibilities, like laundry, phone calls, cleaning, and grocery shopping, so I feel as though my mind, body, and soul are more peaceful. Who doesn't love that feeling, right? I would bet that feeling was more available before digital technology kicked into gear.

> *"Everything has become so easy. It's great that it's*
> *at your fingertips, but I miss those good old days.*
> *And we're connected, but it can be very alienating. There is*
> *this distance between all of us because we're speaking to each*
> *other through cameras and monitors and icons and Emojis."*
> — Rami Malek

When conversations were had in pre-digital technology days, there could be more deliberate focus because there were no smartwatches vibrating on people's wrists, or sounds going off on people's smartphones to redirect interest.

Sure, as humans with complex brains, we can take notice of many things at any given moment that are capable of diverting our attention from what's at hand. Someone walking by, a bright-colored shirt, a bird landing near, a noise, a smell, but in this new school technology world, the number of disruptions has intensified. A study called "The iPhone Effect: The Quality of In-Person Social Interactions in the Presence of Mobile Devices" revealed some of the effects of the mere presence of mobile phones on the nature of face-to-face relations.

In the study, if either participant placed a mobile communication device (e.g., smartphone or a cell phone) on the table or held it in their hand during the course of the ten-minute conversation, the quality of the conversation was rated to be less fulfilling compared with conversations that took place in the absence of mobile devices. The same participants who conversed in the presence of mobile communication devices also reported experiencing lower empathetic concern compared with participants who interacted without distracting digital stimuli in their visual field…. Thus, even without active use, the presence of mobile technologies has the potential to divert individuals from face-to-face exchanges, thereby undermining the character and depth of these connections. Individuals are potentially more likely to miss subtle cues, facial expressions, and changes in the tone of their conversation partner's voice, and have less eye contact when their thoughts are directed to other concerns in the presence of a mobile device. These non-verbal and verbal elements of in-person communication are important for a focused and fulfilling conversation.[20]

Before Wi-Fi became a necessity, people usually went to a coffee shop primarily to have a cup of coffee, and maybe even some casual conversation, keeping open the possibility of connecting with someone new. Now, coffee shops tend to be the places where people gather to further embed themselves in the virtual environment.

In Los Angeles, I remember walking into the Starbucks around the corner from our condo at eleven in the morning before heading to an audition and thinking, "Wow, this feels more like Starbucks corporate headquarters than a coffee shop!" The place was jam-packed, every table filled with a man or woman hunched over their computer, typing away. I wish I could say that was a one-time occurrence, but it was not. Every time I went to grab a coffee from there, a shop full of people were on their computers or phones; very rarely were two friends just having a casual chat or was someone from one table making conversation with someone at another table.

Speaking of some casual conversation, I have to share this funny story with you. Just a few weeks ago, my mother and I went to have breakfast at a diner, and an older gentleman was sitting at a table next to us. The waiter seemed to be familiar with the older gentleman, as he began making friendly conversation with him and asked how he was doing. The

---

20   Misra, Shalini et al. "The iPhone Effect: The Quality of In-Person Social Interactions in the Presence of Mobile Devices." *Environment and Behavior*. 48 (2014). 10.1177/0013916514539755.

gentleman answered quite loudly, "How am I doing? Did you ever have a colonoscopy? Because I just did, and it's not so much the actual procedure but the beforehand that sucks!" Well, my mom and I burst out laughing as did the people at the tables around us who chimed in, agreeing. It was an amazing moment of connection between strangers! Some good ol' school simplicity, in the form of casual conversation, that connected people through the positivity of joy and laughter—sometimes that element gets lost in today's technology shuffle.

This lost element is quite evident to generations born before the digital age. Like I spoke to the wonderful woman who told me her memory of her family dancing the polka, I talk to many seniors and love hearing their stories about what life was like before cellphones were part of the societal norm. I consistently hear the same observation that people were much more approachable, talkative, and not so rude and self-involved. If I am being totally frank here, I would agree that we can all be a little rude sometimes.

When we are so wrapped up in what is happening on the other side of our screens, we tend to miss the small moments right in front of us.

Those moments can be as simple as someone smiling at us but being left hanging because we don't even see it.

As a writer and lover of letters, I feel that nothing is more personal than a handwritten letter besides an in-person conversation. When you break it down, in a handwritten letter there is no digital brain getting between you and the person you are writing to. One person's feelings flow out from their heart, in combination with the thoughts that flow out from their brain, through their hands and fingers, and onto the page. The message then is not just a conglomeration of words on a piece of paper but a personal testament of one person's mind, body, and soul to another.

Consider this thought: How sexy do you think it must have been hundreds of years ago, when letters were a main source of communication, to have a significant other write you a handwritten letter? During the time it took for them to write the letter, you knew you were the *only* thing on their mind, and you could feel their energy through the way they formulated each letter of the alphabet. Talk about intimacy!

Okay, let me ask you something else: When you speak to your significant other or someone you are really into, and they look you right in your eyes and smile as you're telling a story, doesn't your heart melt? Mine is melting as I'm just picturing it. If you feel this way, it's because you feel their focus is solely on *you*, on *your words*, and on you *feeling them feel you*. That is the power of focus and the intimacy it brings when that focus is intentional and singular.

Focus is intimacy.

Michael, who is forty-four years young, told me, "As young boys, we would take a stroll up and down the boardwalk in the summertime looking for girls to talk to because there was no such thing as scrolling on an app to do that." Today "scrolling" is the new "strolling." I'm sure posture was better then, as well, because everyone wasn't always hunched over with their heads down and necks stretched out of alignment to write texts or engage on social media. (My chiropractor says that is the very position that has given us all "military neck," keeping him in business!) Without the virtual world available, people's heads were up and out, actually seeing the world around them.

Now that we are part of the virtual world constantly, the possibilities are endless, but this, my friend, can be both a blessing and a curse. The blessing being that we have more variety than we know what to do with, and the curse being the "decision-fatigue" the variety brings.

Decision-fatigue is the turmoil you go through in making any decision no matter how big or small—from deciding which color socks to wear to deciding which house to buy. Either way, decision-fatigue can be draining!

***The stress of decision-fatigue comes from an inability to choose
because of an over-abundance of choices to choose from.***

Michael and I talk about this all the time because I battle with decision-fatigue big time. Whether it's picking out a shirt in a store or deciding which sunscreen to buy, I waste an embarrassing amount of time and energy deciding. If you have ever encountered decision-fatigue, you understand how irritating it can be for both you and anyone around you. Often, the decision you're trying to make is not even significant, but something inside just won't let you choose.

Then, to add to the curse of endless possibilities from the virtual world, there's the "shiny object syndrome." You know exactly what I'm talking about, don't you? You open a tab on your computer to search "sushi restaurants near me," and next thing you know, ten other tabs are open and you've drifted to looking for the cheapest flights to Bora Bora for a vacation you're not even going to take. Even if your goal was to find the restaurant and close the computer, it's next to impossible because you are bombarded with advertisements that lead your brain down other paths. Before you know it, your anxiety is up as you realize you're stuck inside the virtual world—and you still haven't ordered any sushi for dinner.

There's always somewhere else we need to be or something else we need to be doing, and that is because we can do just about anything.

From the second we wake up, we are driven by technology; we immediately pick up our phones to check email and social media. Then when we try to go to sleep, we can't because our brains won't shut off. In an episode of Brendon Burchard's podcast, *The Brendon Show*, he talks about why picking up our phones right when we wake up is one of the worst things we can do. He says, "It is training your brain first thing in the morning to check out of your life, and check into other people's lives." By stimulating the mind like this before we take the time to be with ourselves, we open the door to feelings of nervousness and scatteredness.

I can relate these feelings to when I walk into a big department store for clothing and get overwhelmed. My heart starts to race because I feel like I don't know where to look first. When I'm at one rack, I'm not even paying attention to it because I'm actually looking over my shoulder to see what else is around. On the flip side, when I'm in a small boutique, with fewer choices, I actually feel calmer. Have you experienced something like this? If so, let that be a reminder to take a breath and find a few moments in your day when you can incorporate some pre-digital technology qualities. This can be something as simple as getting a coffee at a coffee shop and sitting down with that coffee without your phone in hand. You may just find that the small gesture gives you the reset you didn't know you needed.

Reflections Section: *Ol' School Simplicity (Pre-Digital Technology)*

- Take some time to recall a few moments that took your breath away. Then, write down if each of them happened while you were connected or disconnected.

_____

_____

_____

_____

- What are some simple things from the pre-digital technology age you would like to adopt? (Example: Reading actual books instead of e-books, or making playtime for your children mean "create time." Instead of playing video games or with apps on the phone, they have to create something using only arts and crafts supplies.)

_____

_____

_____

_____

- What do you do that brings you joy and peace that has nothing to do with digital technology?

_____

_____

_____

_____

Incorporating the simplistic qualities of pre-digital technology days into our busy lives can remind us that often the most beautiful moments are the simplest ones, and we are capable beings even without our digital friends. In the next chapter, we will discuss specific ways to restore balance to our dependence on new school technology.

Chapter Five:

BALANCING ACT

"In this life, we are in a constant search for inner peace. We long for it in all aspects of our lives, both personally and professionally. The truth is that we cannot have inner peace without balance. It seems that having too much or too little of anything completely throws off our balance, therefore limiting our inner peace."
— Raheem DeVaughn

Now that we've explored this age of technology and looked into the time before digital technology, how do we find our way between these two worlds? We know digital technology isn't going anywhere, so how do we use it without letting it use us? The only answer, my friend, is balance. That priceless word that represents a deep peace we all long for, whether consciously or unconsciously. Balance puts us in control of when and how we want to use digital technology, instead of being puppets with our devices as the puppeteers.

For example, have you ever found yourself picking up your phone in the middle of doing something else to mindlessly scroll through social media? Michael calls finding me with my phone in hand, staring blankly while my fingers swipe away, the "Facebook Stare." That blank face where I appear to be in a *Night of the Living Dead* trance falling down an abyss of wasted time on reality star gossip or the latest vegan face products to hit the market. He immediately says, "Get off of Facebook," and I'm quickly pulled out of my life-sucking daze.

The saddest part is that most of the time this behavior is unconscious. It's as if my hand is magnetically pulled to the phone if there is just one tenth of a second without something actively going on. Do you know this feeling? I know when I am lost in the Facebook stare, I am not even enjoying social media. It's happening out of sheer habit, and what I'm really doing is taking up hours on end doing nothing that adds value to my life, yet I can't pull myself away. Those hours could have been used to write this book, for goodness sake.

Taking Back Control

We are creatures of habit through and through, so let's recognize what habits we've adopted and change them if need be. If you are thinking how much you love social media and see nothing wrong with it, I want you to know I, too, love social media, but when it goes from being a fun hobby or a part of your business to being an addiction, it becomes a problem.

In a 2017 study titled, "Social Networking Sites and Addiction: Ten Lessons Learned," researchers found:

> ...one could claim that it is not an addiction to the technology, but to connecting with people, and the good feelings that 'likes' and positive comments of appreciation can produce. Given that connection is the key function of social networking sites....it appears that 'social networking addiction' may be considered an appropriate denomination of this potential mental health problem.[21]

---

21   Kuss, D. J., Griffiths, M. D. "Social Networking Sites and Addiction: Ten Lessons Learned." *Int J Environ Res Public Health*. 14.3 (2017): 311. doi:10.3390/ijerph14030311.

We only have a finite number of moments in the day, but we get to decide what we do with those moments. When we consciously choose to make new school technology a part of some of those moments, great. By contrast, when we find ourselves agitated because moments on a shopping site turn into hours without our awareness of the time passing, we need to reassess our relationship with technology.

In an NPR interview, *New York Times* tech reporter Matt Richtel said, "When you check your information, when you get a buzz in your pocket, when you get a ring—you get what they call a dopamine squirt. You get a little rush of adrenaline. Well, guess what happens in its absence? You feel bored. You're conditioned by a neurological response: 'Check me check me check me check me.'"[22]

To be completely transparent here, when I am sitting on my butt with my phone in hand swiping away and feeling crappy for doing it, yet unable to break away, addiction is exactly what comes to mind. I get that same out-of-control feeling when I have a piece of chocolate and it's so darn good that I can't help but march right back to the pantry for more.

When I began analyzing how to find more balance in my life by continuing to enjoy the most technological advances while still maintaining my ability to authentically communicate, I imagined it like the "21-day fix" diet that supplies you with different-sized containers for each food group. The purpose of the diet is not to *cut* anything out but to adopt portion control; that's exactly what we want to do with our fixation on devices, social media, and such. We want to fit those fixations into nicely portioned containers. This way we can indulge in them in a healthy way that doesn't take over our lives. How does that sound?

Take a moment to check in with yourself and get really honest about what may have some control over you. TikTok? Hulu? Clubhouse? Please be completely truthful with yourself because, just like any problem, the first step to fixing it is becoming aware of it.

---

22 NPR. "Digital Overload: Your Brain on Gadgets." Last modified August 24, 2010. www.npr.org/templates/story/story.php?storyId=129384107.

Then, have some fun using the containers in the Reflections Section to help you take back control. Remember that everything begins in the mind, so writing inside these containers can encourage the visuals of what you want in your mind's eye. Maybe writing "Family Time" inside the biggest container instead of "Instagram" will flip a switch for you in your brain to help lessen the hold that the application has on you.

Reflections Section: *Taking Back Control*

- Do you ever pick up your phone unconsciously while doing something else and realize a few minutes later that you're not focusing on the task at hand? (Example: In the middle of preparing PowerPoint slides for an important meeting, you pick up the phone to check Twitter.) How did you feel once you realized what you were doing?

_____

_____

_____

- For the sake of true honesty with yourself, what forms of technology do you feel have control over you? (Example: Snapchat, dating apps, video games.)

_____

_____

_____

- What will you put in each of these containers to better balance new school technology with ol' school simplicity? (Example: If Clubhouse, video games, TikTok, and Amazon Prime have you hooked, move them to the smallest four containers, after Physical Activity, Journaling, and Family Time.)

Portion Control Containers

Choosing

In a world of overstimulation, finding balance can seem like a big task, so it takes commitment. That commitment can begin by asking yourself this one question:

> ***Do I care enough about myself and my relationships
> to give the best of myself?***

As hard as honest communication may be at times, the alternatives are much worse, as we've discussed in previous chapters. Let me remind you of the risks: stress, doubt, strained relationships, wasted energy, missed opportunities, and worst of all, wasted time. I'd rather take the honest communication; wouldn't you? Okay, good. So, let's do that by making a commitment and choosing to give the best of ourselves.

Think back to a time when you had a goal and you made it happen. How did you feel when you achieved that goal? What do you think allowed you to achieve that goal as opposed to goals you didn't achieve? Please really analyze these questions for yourself. I'll wait here.

Okay…so I'm going to let you in on a little secret if you didn't already figure it out.

> ***In all of the instances you achieved your goals,***
> ***your want was bigger than your fear.***

That's it. All of your accomplishments come down to this one little statement. Fear will always make a guest appearance, especially when it comes to going for something you want. It's about what you choose to do with that fear. You can let it win by focusing on it, or you can drown out the cries of fear by fiercely focusing on your desired outcome.

For me, writing this book is an example. I knew it was something I needed and wanted to do, but some days, the fear of doing it was intense. So, instead of writing, I would waste time doing the most mundane things. I'd catch myself reorganizing my drawers, analyzing my face in the mirror, singing, or even scrolling away on Instagram—yes, the *very* thing I was supposed to be writing about!

The minute I snapped out of my haze, I quickly remembered the self-judgment and frustration I had felt in the past because of procrastination. Then, I'd put the phone down and get to writing. Before I knew it, the fear subsided and was replaced with a calm power because I knew I was doing what I was meant to. As the moments of realizing I didn't need to procrastinate added up, it became easier to get straight to writing.

All of that said, the first step is simply choosing—choosing to make giving the best of yourself a priority. Do you want to be known as the friend who never calls back or the one who never listens? Do you want to be the team member at work whom everyone dreads working with because your tone in emails is always off-putting, and you never contribute by sharing ideas? Giving the best of yourself means being quite the contrary in those situations.

The mystery of life is we don't know how long we have to live it. Therefore, why would we want to waste time by giving anything less than our best?

I can assure you that once you decide to give the best of yourself, you'll begin operating on a higher plane where your strongest potential lies. By seeing what you are truly made of, you will feel empowered and lead with confidence in all that you do. So, is that a *yes* to giving the best of yourself? Awesome!

"To give anything less than your best, is to sacrifice the gift."
— Steve Prefontaine

Reflections Section: *Choosing*

- Do you care enough about yourself and your relationships to give the best of yourself?

_____

_____

- Think back to a time when you had a goal and made it happen. What was that goal? How did you feel when you achieved it?

_____

_____

_____

- Why do you think you were able to achieve that goal as opposed to ones you didn't achieve?

_____

_____

_____

Identifying

Now that you've made the commitment, it's time to get more specific. The intention is to identify what your soul's desires are. Anything you feel is fair game because this is for *you*. This is a practice in letting go and giving up the need to censor your truest desires. Because of misguided societal beliefs we've adopted, we sometimes feel ashamed of the things we really want. We believe we're undeserving or that our desires are silly, and they *should* be something else.

In my case, I've lived a lot of my life beating myself up by thinking I *should* be doing more, or I *should* do better, or I *should* have handled a situation differently. *Should, should, should, should, should.* I've *should* all over myself! Well "shoulding" is exhausting and terrible, so don't do it. The quicker you take *should* out of your vocabulary, the happier you'll be, trust me. Dig deep and be proud of whatever your soul's desires are.

Maybe your desire is to have the financial abundance to be able to buy your parents a home, to meet the person of your dreams, to own your own bakery, or to be a great mother, father, sister, brother, wife, or husband. Anything goes in this exercise because we're all unique and have unique desires.

After you finish your list, I'd like you to look back at each one individually. Take a moment to think about how each one could be accomplished through strong communication. Look beyond the surface of each desire and think a little bit deeper.

Let's use the example of improving your physical health as a desire. At first look, communication does not come to mind as a means to this end. Eating a more balanced diet and hiring a trainer are more along the lines of what could initially come to mind. When you go a little further with those ideas, though, you can see how communication is still a factor. Eating more balanced meals requires truthful communication with yourself to see where you've gone amiss with your eating habits. Hiring a trainer who understands your specific needs to get you the most benefit from your sessions also requires truthful communication.

In addition, that same communication must be shared with your doctor and/or nutritionist so they have all the information needed to effectively steer you on a better path. If you're not fully communicating with them, you are setting yourself up for disappointment.

I want you to really grasp this idea that communication truly plays a role in every part of your life. I guarantee most of the desires you have written down will have a connection to communication in one way or another.

Reflections Section: *Identifying*

Column One What are your soul's desires?	Column Two How can they be reached with strong communication?
_____	_____
_____	_____
_____	_____
_____	_____
_____	_____

Scheduling

"Never leave the scene of a decision, without scheduling in a commitment that guarantees fulfillment."
— Tony Robbins

Once you've made your list, take out what you use to schedule for the week.

Side note: If you're like me, you use the calendar on your phone for scheduling appointments and adding reminders. The problem is the calendar shares a space with everything that distracts me—social media apps, email, and shopping sites. My initial intention is always straightforward—open the calendar and add a reminder or an appointment. Unfortunately, once the phone is in hand, the temptation is too strong. The next thing I know, I'm taking a quiz on Facebook to find out which flower I'd be if I were a flower. So, if you're anything like me, please use an actual planner, whether it be a small one or one with more space that you can write in.

Take out that planner now, and if you don't have one, please purchase one today so you can make paper scheduling a new habit. For now, use a blank piece of paper. In the planner/on the paper, write in specific times to use ol' school simplicity each week based on the desires you wrote down.

Some may say, "Ugh, I have enough things to schedule. I don't want to schedule every moment." My response is, "Change your perspective." Look at the big picture and realize that you're training yourself to value and practice ol' school simplicity, which takes the complexity out of your communication with others, thus making your life *less* complicated.

> ***When you use ol' school simplicity, you propel yourself forward to attaining your soul's desires.***

Maybe you went through a rough divorce and are estranged from your child. Your desire is to be more present, but you live and work on the opposite side of the country. Pick a time (even if it's just ten minutes) to talk to your child and record that day and time in your planner as if it's an appointment for work. Then as things get better, those scheduled phone calls may become scheduled in-person visits. If one of your desires is work-related, this still applies.

Maybe your desire is to move up in the company you work for, but you haven't brought it up out of fear of what your boss will say. I challenge you to schedule a time this week to talk to your boss. If they are someone who only interacts through email, that's okay; just step up to the plate! Write an email saying you would like to speak in person when they have some free time. This request a) shows your boss you are a confident employee taking the initiative, and b) increases your confidence by proving to yourself you can overcome fear and open the door to making a change.

If one of your desires is to become a better friend, then schedule in a phone call or a quick meet up to check-in with that friend each week. Of course, life happens and can prevent you from accomplishing what you've scheduled at the exact time you planned, but the goal is to follow that schedule as much as you can.

Holding ourselves accountable is how we build new habits, and we can do that through scheduling.

Knowing what you want, why you want it, and how to make it happen is essential to meeting your desires. I have realized how often I think and talk about what I desire, but then I waste time doing things that have nothing to do with that desire. Do you have dreams or goals you go on and on about in conversation, yet you never take action to move toward them? In the past, I have felt my dreams were being safely kept alive in the arms of my words, so I didn't need to rock the boat and risk failure by taking steps to bring them to fruition. You too, huh?

I've realized through the process of writing this book that *talking* about taking action is easy, whereas actually taking the action—focused action—is the challenge.

Talking without taking focused action is a common habit and the reason many of us miss out on opportunities.

We waste time when we only talk and/or take unintentional actions.

In the interest of taking focused action to become master communicators, write down some unintentional, unfocused actions you tend to practice regularly that distract you from reaching your goals.

Reflections Section: *Scheduling*

* Take out your paper scheduler and schedule some ol' school simplicity time. (If you don't have a planner yet, order one today.) You

can start with just two half-hour sessions for this week, but make the sessions for those who have a connection to one of your desires. (Example: Call your business partner to talk over plans for the new product you're launching; call your aunt to check on her and her health; call your doctor's office to schedule your annual physical.) After you're finished writing those times in your scheduler, also write them here for secondary accountability.

———————————————————————————————

———————————————————————————————

———————————————————————————————

———————————————————————————————

• Write down some unintentional, unfocused actions you catch yourself taking daily that distract you from reaching your goals. (Example: Texting memes back and forth with a friend, watching hours of TV, taking quizzes on Facebook.)

———————————————————————————————

———————————————————————————————

———————————————————————————————

———————————————————————————————

Systematizing

To create more communication balance in our lives, having systems in place is especially imperative. I like to use the word "systems" instead of "rules" because the word rules reminds me of my Catholic school days when there was a lot of fear attached to the word. Systems are meant to evoke confidence, not fear. They give us confidence by providing us with a structure that keeps the focus of our goals sharp. If you're in a relationship, maybe you already have some systems in place.

Let me provide an illustration of a system from my own relationship. In the past, when Michael would drive with me in the passenger seat, I automatically picked up my phone and started scrolling away. Well, one day we were with friends at a birthday party when Michael picked up his phone to check email for a few minutes. The fact that we were in the middle of a social event when he did this bothered me immensely! So, naturally, when we left the party, I had *no* problem communicating that to him, and we ended up in an argument. In the midst of our argument, he said, "You're mad because I needed to check something important in my email; meanwhile, every time we drive somewhere, you're on that phone the entire time! Talk about a hypocrite!" He was 100 percent right. How dare I get annoyed with him when I constantly waste precious time with him by getting caught up in the virtual world.

The two of us being in the car together is a blessing because it gives us the time to talk, reminisce, plan, laugh, question, and connect. Robbing ourselves of that time by worrying about what others are doing on social media is ludicrous. The beauty of this argument was that it made me realize how important it is to be present when Michael and I are alone. How great is that?

The argument led us to create a system where we put our phones away while we're in the car together. It is one of the best decisions we've ever made.

Before we drove across the country from California to New Jersey, many people told us that after a few days we would be on each other's last nerve. However, we didn't turn the radio on once and talked the entire way back. We laughed nonstop, played the "Gratitude Game," listing all of the things in our lives we are grateful for, and we talked about our dreams. It was one of the best trips we've ever taken, and we got back to New Jersey feeling closer than ever. A deeper connection was built because we had a system in place that allowed us to use our valuable time wisely.

Let me offer you another instance when having a system in place was extremely beneficial. I explained earlier how challenging it could be to sit down and write when I don't have the option of being by the beach with just me and the seagulls. It is easy to get pulled away if I don't use the system I put in place for myself, which is called the "One Hour Airplane Mode." I put the phone in airplane mode to avoid any distractions and give myself one hour at a time to write.

I chose one hour because, in the past, I'd try to overachieve by writing for longer, but all I achieved was forced creativity and sitting in the same spot for too long. In turn, I needed a new system. Now, I get excited about sitting down for that hour because it's only one hour and I know that a break isn't too far off. Then I can make a phone call, write some emails, grab food, or change the laundry. This takes the pressure off, which frees up my mind to relax into the flow of writing.

As I write this, I realize my laundry has been sitting wet in the washer for over two hours. Good thing I only have ten more minutes until a break.

Reflections Section: *Systematizing*

- What are a couple of systems you can put in place for yourself and/or a relationship to balance new school technology with ol' school simplicity?

_____

_____

_____

_____

Now that you have committed to saying yes to giving the best of yourself, identified your soul's desires and realized how strong communication is tied to those desires, scheduled ol' school simplicity time, and created systems for balance, you've already stepped into the shoes of becoming a master communicator.

To help you walk in those shoes that you've stepped into, I will be giving you more specific practices to balance new school technology with ol' school simplicity as we move forward on our journey. First, though, we're going to dive into how to stay flexible and adaptable when circumstances beyond our control happen and how to make the absolute best of communicating virtually!

Chapter Six:
ROLLIN' WITH THE TIMES

"Everything is figureoutable."
— Marie Forleo

I've written much of this book during the COVID-19 pandemic, which is quite ironic because I've explained how meeting with someone in person and feeling their energy is the most direct and transparent way to communicate. Yet, this is the one way to connect that we *can't* take part in due to the circumstances, so does this mean we *can't* have authentic communication until this is all over?

Absolutely not! This means we're being called to level up in our lives and adapt as master communicators, by learning how to communicate *even more* distinctly through virtual means. In writing this book during this time, I've had to find other ways to master my communication without being in person, so I could help you to do the same. In other words, writing this book during this time is not ironic but divine timing.

Recently, when I had the honor of co-hosting the first-ever virtual "World Summit" created by Tony Robbins and Dean Graziosi, I was able to witness what becomes possible when you turn a seemingly impossible situation into a new opportunity. The event was originally scheduled to be in person in Las Vegas, but since that was no longer an option with the pandemic, they could either cancel the event or find another way. They chose the latter. They held the event in a space that Robbins had created months prior, when his event "Unleash the Power Within" couldn't be held in person and he needed to find a way to still reach thousands of people to help transform their lives. By continuing to look for a solution, he had a 360-degree arena completely surrounded with screens built. He and Graziosi decided to use that arena for the "World Summit." In addition to themselves, there were eight incredible speakers featured at the three-day event: Russell Brunson, Jamie Kern Lima, Trent Shelton, Jenna Kutcher, Brendon Burchard, Pete Vargas, Pat Quinn, and Bari Baumgardner. These speakers all shared their stories as knowledge brokers and delivered their strategies to more than 9,000 people all over the world through Zoom.

As Karissa Kouchis and I introduced the speakers, shared our personal stories, and kept everyone watching energized, we, like the speakers, were able to connect with those people as if we were in the same room with them. We observed people's spirits come alive as they listened to the speakers and made emotional breakthroughs. Those breakthroughs were able to happen thanks to the power of technology. By looking for solutions to a seemingly impossible situation, a new opportunity to reach thousands of people arose.

When your back is up against the wall, but you keep looking for solutions, a new path will be created!

By looking at any challenging time from the perspective of "How can I grow?" you can use the time to reflect, release, and refocus. This perspective lets you understand that challenges offer you an unexpected chance to become a better version of yourself and affect those in your intimate and business life more positively. This case of the pandemic allows for a crash course in skills we're going to have to learn anyway because our world's rapidly changing due to advanced technology. Why not learn now, right?

Businesses that have never operated virtually must learn to do so if they want to keep running, and friends and family members who want to stay as connected as possible must tap into the virtual world to experience that connection. Hopping on a Zoom, Skype, or Facetime call is the closest thing we have to being "in person," so we must know how to do this effectively and with confidence.

Okay, so with all of that said, right now it is about putting our best foot forward by learning how to operate in the virtual world.

Virtual Etiquette

In my many recent Zoom group and one-on-one coaching calls, I have already witnessed individuals dealing with a wide variety of communication setbacks. Some users do not turn their cameras on, denying the extra level of connection that seeing a person's body language offers, and others have their cameras on, but their focus is elsewhere. Speaking to my clients through the lens of my computer, I have seen some of them texting, others watching television, and others simply engaging with other people who are in the room.

Let me offer you an instance of this. I was hosting a group coaching call for a company training session with about twenty people. In the meeting, I was giving them advice on how to communicate genuinely with their clients. As I spoke, I began to suspect a few of the people were not aware I could see them. One woman decided to go about her nightly routine, brushing her long, picturesque hair right in front of the camera, and using it as a mirror, while another woman brought me to dinner with her. She listened half-heartedly to my earnest messages, as she nonchalantly sat down with her computer to eat with her entire family. There I was, virtually in the middle of what appeared to be a delicious family dinner, as I continued to speak in complete disbelief. Now, I tell you this not only to make you chuckle but to make you aware that this is where "Virtual Etiquette" comes into play.

You must treat your video calls and virtual meetings as you would "in person" meetings. Do you think it is respectful not to look someone in the eye when they are talking to you from across a table because you're watching other people walk by? How about half-listening because you are texting someone else or scrolling on your phone as the person you're meeting with is mid-conversation? What about your attention span reaching its limit, making your eyes glaze over with boredom, letting the other person know you've checked out?

I have faith that your answer to all of those examples is no. With that said, I'd like you to understand that this same idea of respect applies to our new normal way of communicating. Respecting one another's time and energy is essential, and that respect happens through focus. Focusing on the person speaking, and letting everything else take a backseat. When we narrow our focus, we not only respect the other person, but we respect ourselves by giving ourselves the chance to learn and grow through listening completely.

When it comes to Zoom, we don't have to use video. That is totally okay *as long as* we let the host of the group know beforehand. This gives the host a heads up of what to expect. Otherwise, not being forewarned that someone will not be on video can be a bit jarring.

For example, during my first Zoom call ever, I hosted four people. Because one of them was not on video, I noticed my energy was thrown off. When I can see someone, I feel much more connected to them and have a more forward energy than when I am talking to a blank screen. As a result, I felt odd because only three of the four were seen. This person had every right to be off camera, but because nothing was said beforehand, I expected the camera to go on at any second. As I've learned how to use this application better, I've realized I could have simply asked if they would be on camera, and if they had said no, I would have felt so much better. So, if this happens to you, remember to just ask. (You know, communicate authentically—like I've been driving home this entire journey…ha-ha.)

When hosting a Zoom meeting, think of it as hosting a party.

When you host a party, and you prefer your guests take their shoes off, you just tell them. If you need your guests to bring wine or dessert, you let them know. If you don't need them to bring anything, you let them know that too. Similarly, when hosting a Zoom meeting, if you would prefer to have everyone have their sound muted when they enter, let them know. If you would like them to raise their hands to speak in the group, let them know. If you will be recording the entire meeting, make sure to tell them that so if they are uncomfortable being recorded, you are aware. If you will be taking breaks to answer questions, encourage the members to use the chat box for their questions.

Please understand, leading a Zoom meeting in this way is meant to inspire structure. When we practice structure and etiquette within our virtual communities, our communication becomes easier, simpler, and clearer. What is better than that? Once again, we avoid wasting those two power players in our lives—time and energy—and instead, we get to what matters. Whether that be connecting with loved ones or sharing information for work, we escape the detours and get right to it.

Here are a few other tips to consider while you are on video calls or in virtual meetings.

1. **Body Position.** Find a comfortable spot where you can be seated or standing and still. So often, I get on a call where the person on the other end is walking around, or driving, and the camera is going all over the place. This not only makes the person watching dizzy, but it makes it nearly impossible for either party to be fully focused on the conversation. I understand sometimes you don't have a choice and have to be en route during a meeting, but if you have the option of being in one spot, please choose that.

2. **Lighting.** Find a location in your home or otherwise with great lighting. Great lighting makes everything better as you know

when you take a photo. Facing a window during the day or using a ring light will provide the lighting you need. The purpose of a video is to see one another, so make sure your lighting assists in that purpose.

3. **Camera Angle.** You want to feel like you're looking directly into the eyes of who is on the other side of your screen and vice versa. The way to do that is to position the camera so the lens is in line with your eyes or slightly above. You can accomplish this by placing your computer on top of a box or stacked books. Trust me, this doesn't have to be fancy. You can make it work with what you have at home. If you're on your phone, you can lean the phone against a windowsill or purchase a small, flexible tripod stand. This way, you can put the phone on the stand, and if you need more height, place the stand on top of some boxes or books. Many ring lights already have a camera holder for the phone as well.

4. **Sound.** Find a location with good sound. When the television or the comings and goings of our lives can be heard, it's a struggle to focus on calls. It's enough to deal with the inconsistencies of Wi-Fi and screens freezing left and right. We don't need to add weak sound to the mix. I suggest going into different rooms to discover which has the best sound. Sometimes, the best sound is in odd places you wouldn't think of, but anywhere is okay as long as you can be heard. Ask a friend to call you so they can help you figure out which location provides the clearest sound. That's what friends are for, right?

5. **Attire.** On a video call or in any virtual meeting, especially for a professional purpose, please remember to be presentable. As comfortable as you may feel lying in bed in your pajamas, with the computer on your lap, it's pretty awkward for the other people there; it feels like they've walked in on you in your bedroom, in a private moment, and that's not cool. If you're wondering if people actually do this, the answer is, yes. So, before you put your, "I'm

alone and don't need to be presentable" clothes on, ask yourself, "Would I wear this to a face-to-face meeting?" If the answer is no, put some decent clothes on, will ya? When deciding on what to wear, you can use these three simple guidelines and call a friend or loved one over to help you find attire that makes you feel great in your skin but is the least distracting. 1) Wear what makes you feel powerful and professional yet comfortable. 2) Wear either solid colors or the least patterns you can find. 3) Wear no logos. Remember, you want to keep others' focus on what you're *saying* and not on what you're *wearing*.

6. **Background.** Do your best to be on video in front of a simple background. This means avoiding busy-looking paintings behind you, different picture frames, a kitchen full of dishes and cups lying around, or anything to pull the attention away from you. We can be easily distracted, so wherever you can find that has the smallest chance to distract, the better. I love filming in front of a blank, solid-colored wall to make it easy, but if you don't have a solid wall, go with a background with the least number of items, or purchase a plain backdrop online that you can put up when you're on video. I know many people use virtual backgrounds, but I find that those too can be distracting because people often choose ones that are really interesting to look at, which makes everyone look at *the background*. Also, when you move in front of a virtual background, it often looks like you're in a video game, and you want your video calls/virtual meetings to feel as much like you're in person as possible.

These tips can be applied anywhere in the virtual communication world, so to connect most effectively, remember to use them. Even on the audio platform, Clubhouse, you're not seen, but you are heard, so use the points that apply. When moderating a room, just like with Zoom, remind yourself that it's just like hosting a party. Give the room members, your "guests," as much information as possible, from who you are and what the conversation's theme is to the rules of how the room will run. When you're a member of the audience or brought to the stage, treat those experiences like you're a guest at someone else's party. Don't be afraid to take part in the fun and socialize at the party by raising your hand to ask a question or add value, but also show respect to the host and other guests by finding a spot with good sound where the room can hear you well when you speak, and muting your microphone when not speaking.

When we practice these "Virtual Etiquette" tips, we express ourselves in the best possible state. In other words, we say yes to virtually giving the best of ourselves.

Through a challenging event like a pandemic with so many people separated from their loved ones and communication happening mostly behind screens, a newfound appreciation for ol' school simplicity will be born. Once we can be in person, the first thing we'll want to do is meet up with our friends and family, and we'll welcome in-depth conversations where we can touch hands or give hugs. There will also be a new sense of gratitude for new school technology and a pure recognition of its ability to keep us connected despite physical separation. In other words, seeing the value of both of these worlds right in front of our eyes can become the ultimate catalyst for learning to balance them.

Reflections Section: *Virtual Etiquette*

- Which of the "Virtual Etiquette" tips have you not thought about, that you will begin to apply immediately?

_____

_____

_____

Finding Comfort in the Virtual World

*"It's only after you've stepped outside of your comfort zone
that you begin to change, grow, and transform."*
— Roy T. Bennett

Each of us has our own comfort zone. It is the place we are most familiar with, the one where we feel most at ease because we are safe in knowing what it looks like, what it feels like, and what to expect there. There are no surprises inside the comfort zone because we've spent so much time there that nothing throws us off of our center.

As humans, we like to try to control everything, and when we're inside our comfort zone, that control feels possible because we're able to manage what we already know to anticipate. Being comfortable is something we all love because, let's face it, being comfortable feels amazing. You still own those twelve-year-old white sweatpants, even though they have turned yellow and look slightly offensive because they're so comfortable. You drive the same route to work, even though the dreary views make you feel miserable. Although you know the other route is more scenic and will make you happier, you'd rather not have to learn new directions. You date the same person for years because you're comfortable with them. Even though you know they are not "the one," it is way better than putting yourself out there in the dating pool and risking a broken heart.

How about never really going for what your true, heartfelt, soul-calling dream is because you're more comfortable in a job you hate than you would be to pursue what you love and chance possible failure? See, feeling comfortable is a double-edged sword because comfort is necessary for certain moments but definitely not for all moments. When we have had a long, hard day at work and we just want to get into our fluffy pajamas and veg out on the couch, *that* is when comfort is necessary. When we start a new career and need to learn completely new skills, we don't need comfort. In fact, the opposite is needed—the feeling of expansion and being stretched beyond what we are accustomed to.

When we stay in our comfort zone, we may feel safe, but in reality, we are stagnant. We are hiding our fear of growth behind a mask of contentment.

Growing and expanding is the antithesis of being comfortable—stepping outside of our comfort zone is where the full beauty of life resides. Yes, that includes uncertainty, failure, and letting go of what we thought we knew. This process can be scary, but it is where the transformation happens. To get many of the things we say we want, we must go through some pain, and that pain can be physical, emotional, spiritual, or all three.

Think about Rocky Balboa in *Rocky IV*. His best friend, Apollo Creed, gets killed in an exhibition fight with the Russian machine, Ivan Drago. Being the honorable man he is, Rocky cannot let his friend's death be in vain, so he decides he must fight Drago. Balboa goes from being on the verge of retirement to training harder than ever before, while he is older than ever before. Do you think he felt comfortable and pain-free having to wake up in the wee hours of the morning to train in the snow of a foreign country? Do you think there was no emotional pain knowing that even if he won, that wouldn't bring his best friend back? See, what makes this movie, and all of the Rocky movies, in my Rocky-loving opinion, so poignant is we see the pain and discomfort Rocky endures to achieve his goal, and we know there's no way around it. As the audience, we recognize that the discomfort is the exact component necessary for Rocky to transform into whom he needs to become. That same discomfort is what we, too, need to transform into whom we want to become.

> *"Goin' in one more round when you don't think you can—*
> *that's what makes all the difference in your life."*
> — Rocky Balboa

Growing up as a dancer, I started studying only tap and jazz until my dance teacher explained that I needed to take ballet to increase my overall technique for all dance styles. I took her advice, and even though I wasn't the biggest fan of ballet and using my body in that way was uncomfortable, I got my booty to that ballet barre. Every day, my muscles ached and I went home with bloody feet from working in pointé shoes to make my feet stronger. My precious grandmother, who I called "Franny Panties," would fill a bucket of warm water and soap for me to soak my feet in, and then she would wrap them before I went to bed, only for me to wake up the next day to go through all of the pain once again. As tough as bloody toes and tears from the physical and emotional pain of pushing myself were, all the discomfort was worth what I gained. I became a well-rounded dancer who went on to have a long career as a professional performing artist on Broadway and other mediums.

Think about a time when you went beyond what was familiar and tried something new—a time when you learned a new language or an instrument. What about a time when you ran that extra mile on the treadmill? Even though you wanted to vomit, the pride you felt from pushing past your limit was stronger than any other sensation. As you remind yourself of these times, also remember that they were initially uncomfortable.

> *"People who are successful are not only willing to get uncomfortable, but they know they have to make a habit of it if they want to stay successful."*
> — Jen Sincero

At first attempt, any new skill is unfamiliar; it challenges you, probably causes a lot of frustration, and can make you feel incompetent. That discomfort is the result of stepping outside of your comfort zone and walking into new territory. We all have a choice. We can decide it's too hard and we're going to crawl back to the safety of our comfort zone or we can continue facing the hardships to reap the benefits on the other side. When we choose to continue in the face of unfamiliarity, we find that little by little, we become more and more competent and confident. Then, before we know it, we have grasped something that was once foreign to us, and most importantly, we have shown ourselves what we are capable of!

If we can change our perspective to see pain and hardships
as signposts to our greatest potential, rather than traps
to run away from, we will boldly step out of our comfort zone.

My mother, Ona, and I were just talking on the phone, and I told her about this chapter. When I read her what I had written so far, we agreed she likes to remain in her comfort zone. Whenever she is asked about trying something new, her first answer is always no. She feels safe in a routine, even if that routine isn't bringing her much joy or excitement. But I have discovered, as her daughter, whom she trusts completely, that she always has the best time when I give her a little push. In the moment of that push, what happens is she doesn't have the time to let her negative mind get in the way because I give her no choice to say no. Before she even realizes it, she is having a great time and standing in her joy. "Let's go, Mom. We're trying this new restaurant," or "Come on, Mom; hop on the flight and come see me in California," or "I like that style dress. It's different than anything else you've ever worn." Whatever the situation, when my mother just says, yes, even with hesitation at first, she is never disappointed.

A few years back, my parents, Michael, and I went to Cape May, New Jersey, to celebrate my mom's big seventieth birthday. We stayed at a gorgeous bed and breakfast where we had wine and cheese at 5:00 p.m., overlooking the beach, before heading out for her birthday dinner. The four of us got all dressed up and had a wonderful dinner full of great conversation, laughter, and delicious food. Afterward, we had no plans, but as we were driving around the quaint town, Michael thought we should play mini-golf. Right away, in true Ona fashion, my mother said, "No. Get out of here. I'm not playing mini-golf!"

"Oh, yes you are," Michael said, and before she knew it, we were parked and walking to the window to pay and grab our clubs. Well, from her first swing, the smile never left her face. Not only were we all crying from laughing so much, but Ona-baby came out in first place, kicking all our butts after many effortless holes in one.

By saying yes to as many new experiences as possible, stepping outside of our comfort zone will become a habit we look forward to.

As humans, we all crave comfort, and our natural tendency is to stay in that comfort, but doing so is what holds us back. When we stay in that zone, we do not grow, change, or have experiences we would have had if we stepped outside of those perimeters.

Many of us are not even *aware* that we are avoiding life by remaining inside our comfort zones because we've gotten so comfortable in them. If this statement describes you, or someone you know whom you think would be open to a new perspective, read this chapter again or give it to them to read.

It only makes sense that when you dip your toe outside of the boundaries of your comfort zone into the ocean of the unknown, it will be uncomfortable at first.

See, the real fun starts outside of our comfort zone because we don't know what we are capable of until we try. For many people, the world of virtual meetings and seeing someone through a phone is still very unusual. They associate a phone with the ears, not the eyes. So, when someone like my mother hears me say, "You can see me on the phone," it make no sense to her—the association is set in her brain. The only way to change that association is by creating a new one through practice and repetition.

My mom now gets video calls from some family members and me, so she is becoming more familiar with the idea. I am not going to sit here and tell you that Facetime is now her favorite thing in the world, but she is stepping outside of her comfort zone more frequently, so she is seeing the benefits. My mother now gets to see Michael and me when we cannot be with her in person, and we're able to show her things like the backyard that he has been working on. Slowly but surely, she is making a new association in her mind to connect the phone with not only the ears, but the eyes, too.

If you have a family member who refuses to roll with the times, help them out a bit by sitting with them and giving them a little tutorial on how it works. While your family member is watching, call a friend and let your family member know it is just like a phone call, but instead of raising the phone to your ear, you hold it away from you and look at the screen. That's all.

Having to explain how a video call works may seem silly to some, but remember that not every generation was brought up in the digital age. I believe it is our job as friends and family to help bridge the gap for those who find digital technology unnatural. Sometimes the problem for those who struggle with technology is it seems too complicated, so they don't want to deal with it. If you show them how simple it really is, they are more apt to try it.

Take some time to answer the questions below. As hard as it may be to admit you've been hiding inside your comfort zone, it will be just as freeing once you become aware you are in there and start working on getting out. We all struggle with hiding inside our comfort zone, to one degree or another, so don't be ashamed or feel alone. We are all in this together, so let these questions guide you. Be as candid with yourself as you can. Once you answer the questions, celebrate your honesty because it means you are one step closer to getting enchanted by the magic of life outside of your comfort zone.

Reflections Section: *Finding Comfort in the Virtual World*

- How are you holding yourself back by being too comfortable? In what areas? Relationships? Work life? Personal development? (Examples: Staying in a romantic relationship with someone you're not truly happy with because you're scared to start over. Staying in a job that drains your soul because you're petrified of failing at your dream to start your own company. Backing out of a half-marathon with all of your best friends because you're afraid of training that hard.)

_____

_____

_____

_____

_____

- Describe a time when you went past the edge of your comfort zone. How did you feel once you pushed past the pain and got to the other side?

_____

_____

_____

_____

_____

- What can you do today to step outside of your comfort zone? (Examples: Wear a new color, try a new vegetable, take yourself out to lunch if eating alone scares you, or book a trip to another state or country to see a family member you haven't seen.)

_____

_____

_____

_____

Moving Forward

"Yes to everything scary. Yes to everything that takes me out of my comfort zone. Yes to everything that feels like it might be crazy."
— Shonda Rhimes

Okay, so now that we have talked about "Virtual Etiquette" and finding comfort in the virtual world, it's time for *you* to practice becoming a video call aficionado. Getting comfortable in the virtual world will only serve you personally and professionally because the virtual world is here to stay. Make a vow to yourself to have at *least* one video conversation a day. Even if you fear getting on video calls, *do it anyway.*

Courage isn't courage without fear!

Participating in a video call once a day builds the muscle we need to become comfortable in front of the camera and be ourselves. Think about this—if we can get to the point where we feel completely relaxed and confident on video calls, we set ourselves up for lots of wins in the future. When the time comes for a first Zoom meeting with your boss, you will feel at ease in the setting because you've already taken part in several Zoom calls. Therefore, you won't be nervous—at least about the technology—so you can wholly listen to what your boss has to say and express *exactly* what you need to express.

If a friend is going through a tough time and needs support, you will automatically know to find a quiet spot with no distractions so you can support them. The goal here, my friend, is to become so familiar with the virtual world that being on video becomes second nature.

Have you noticed that when you're familiar with someone, you are much calmer around them so you are naturally more authentic? Well, by becoming familiar with the virtual world, you give yourself the chance to be your most authentic self, and that is the biggest win of all.

All that said, practice makes progress, so let's start right now. I have a challenge for you, and I urge you to start applying it today. When someone sends you a text message, instead of responding with another text, I would like you to respond with a short video. This does a few things. First, it gets you into the habit of being on video beyond when you *have* to, like for a work meeting.

Second, it helps you become familiar with the *feeling* of being on video, which, if you're not used to, can feel quite jarring and weird. When you become familiar with the feeling of being on video, your guard begins to come down when you partake in video calls and virtual meetings, and your real self can shine through.

Third, videos are much more personal than texts and a nice surprise for the person on the other end. Even if the initial text you received was very basic, send the video in response. If you are already comfortable with video calls and love doing them, still send the video. The point of this challenge is to keep making progress in being our most authentic selves in the virtual world; no matter how easy this may be for you already, there is always room for progress.

Reflections Section: *Moving Forward*

- Will you accept the challenge to send a video message as a reply to a text message you receive today?

_____

- *Bookmark this page, and come back later today to answer:* When you sent the video response, how did you feel doing it? How did the other person respond?

_____

_____

_____

The more you apply the "Virtual Etiquette" tips to your virtual communication channels, the more well-defined your communication in those channels becomes. Then, by making stepping outside of your comfort zone a new practice for yourself, you will begin to gain more and more confidence by proving to yourself your capabilities. Consequently, that confidence will carry over into all of your conversations, making you feel entirely comfortable to be yourself communicating, whether it's behind a screen or in person.

Now, it's game time! These next two chapters are full of sensible and straightforward practices to assist you in becoming a master communicator. These are everyday tools that you can apply immediately. Even if some of them are out of your comfort zone, you know what that means: more reason to do them! You have come so far already on our journey, so remain open and willing as we head into the last few chapters, and have a great time with these practices! They are game-changers.

Chapter Seven:

DISCONNECTING TO RECONNECT
(PRACTICES PART 1)

"Be the change you wish to see in the world."
— Mahatma Gandhi

The above quote is truly one of my favorites, and one I carry with me always. Too often, I have found myself upset by other people's actions, especially when it comes to communicating. Whether it's a refusal to have a sit-down talk in the middle of a dispute or simply not communicating at all, a lack of authentic communication has caused me a good amount of stress. When I was younger, I would just get angry and jump to judging the person who wasn't communicating with me. I even wrote a song called "Communicate," which arose out of that anger. As I've grown up, I have come to understand the true meaning of Gandhi's quote that I love so much, which is:

I need to initiate the change I want others to make.

I've often thought I could change people, but the truth is the only person I can change is me. Therefore, if I take a step toward change, maybe it will inspire others to do the same. Also, who am I to judge when I have taken shortcuts in communicating myself? Remember when I told you how I confidently let Michael know when we were dating how not being able to communicate was a deal breaker for me? Years later, he likes to call me out every now and then for doing exactly what I judged him for. "Oh, isn't this funny? Ms. Communication doesn't want to communicate, huh?" With a slight head-shake in shameful agreement, all I can say to that is, "*Touché*, Mike. *Touché*."

While thinking about this chapter, a thought popped into my head that I instinctually knew needed to be a part of this book:

It's easy to take the easy way out.

We have an unlimited supply of helpers to make life easier. These helpers, of course, are the unlimited digital devices that assist us in just about anything we need. The chain of events usually happens like this: We hire (buy) the helper, and we are immediately blown away by how productive they are. We cannot believe how quickly and systematically they get things done. Soon, we find ourselves delegating everything to the helper because they are invincible, as if they're not even human. Oh, wait, that's because they're *not* human. Then, one day, the unthinkable happens. Our helper gets sick and cannot come to work. As much as we beg and plead for them to come in, they are too ill; they can barely get off the couch, never mind do their job. This means *we* have to do our own work. No!

All of a sudden, the tide turns and we're in a panic because we have forgotten how to do everything we've delegated to our helper. We call customer service, figuring we'll get someone on the phone to remind us of what we've forgotten. But guess what? We get connected to another non-human helper, but they can't understand our request because they hear some background noise, so we have to repeat ourselves twenty times. This call, which was supposed to be brief, ends up taking forty-five minutes, and just before we rip our hair out, we hang up and turn to the last resort—relearning on our own.

See, on the surface, delegating to helpers makes our life easier, but deep down, it's stunting our human potential by wasting the mental muscles that must be flexed to experience growth. I think of this when I use a calculator to do all my math. Even though I know at my core that if I just *made* myself figure it out, I could, I don't want to waste the time when I don't need to. Then when the calculator is not working and I have to figure it out, I feel frustrated with myself because I'm an intelligent woman who is taking nine years to multiply.

> *"Just as there is a physical price to always relying on the*
> *technology of the elevator instead of taking the stairs,*
> *so is there a price for lazy mental muscles. Use it or lose it."*
> — Jim Kwik

Here, my friend, lies the Catch-22 of digital technology. If we didn't have these advances, we'd *have* to find a way to do many things on our own, which would push us to use our potential. Technology is convenient, but it also causes our minds to become stagnant in certain areas, just like a plant will wither if it's not watered. This Catch-22 is a major reason learning to balance new school technology with ol' school simplicity is so imperative. We want to be able to discern when and where to delegate, and that will happen through several diverse practices. These practices will be explored in these next two chapters.

Here's the deal. Practice is an integral part of changing our habits, but if there is no drive or passion behind that practice, our old habits will remain. When I was growing up, my dance teacher and mentor used to tell us, "Practice doesn't make perfect. *Perfect* practice makes perfect." Let's use dance as an example. If I had an important performance coming up and rehearsed every day by going through the motions without fully executing the moves ("marking" as performers call it), I would be preparing my muscles to work that way. Then, when the day of the actual performance arrived, and I needed to be "full out," I wouldn't be able to because I failed to make being full out a habit. My muscle memory would only know the half-hearted way I trained, which means, yes, I practiced, but not perfectly because it wasn't to my fullest potential. In this sense, perfect doesn't mean "without any mistakes" but "putting forth your utmost effort."

When I was on the twenty-fifth anniversary tour of the musical *Cats*, I had to put this idea into action. I was a swing for the show, covering six different roles. That meant if any of those six people were out sick, I was in their role for that performance. The musical is intense in every sense of the word, with dancing that is extremely specific and strenuous, singing that displays a wide range and is done while dancing, and crawling around the stage like a cat, which may sound hilarious, but is quite difficult. To top that all off with some hot fudge, whip cream, and a nice cherry, we had to wear layers upon layers of thick makeup, a one-piece unitard, and then fur from head to toe. At the end of the night, you could wring the sweat out of your costume as if you had taken a two-and-a-half-hour shower.

The most challenging part about being a swing, besides having to know several different roles at once, is you are not onstage every night, so you don't have the consistency to develop the stamina needed for the show. Being a performer is just like being an athlete. An athlete needs to constantly train the muscles they'll be using for their sport, so when it's game time, they are ready. The more they train, and the more games they play, the more stamina they have. Well, the same holds true for performers.

Performers rehearse and rehearse to train their bodies, voices, and minds to be ready for showtime. Then during performances, the added elements of the lights, sound, orchestra, and the audience all come together to get the adrenaline pumping through the veins, increasing the performer's stamina with every show. In my case, during rehearsals, because I was a swing and because there was not enough space in the studio, I had to learn the show on the sidelines. I had to do my best to get the moves engrained in my body and find ways to build my stamina.

Here is where my dance teacher's advice came into play in a big way. I realized early on that this was going to be a huge undertaking for me as a performer. Learning six roles for an intense show where I didn't have the space to embody the moves was going to be next level hard, so I became resourceful. I used every spare moment to go through the choreography in the rehearsal room when everyone stepped away for a break. I came in early each day to stretch and dance the choreography and went through my notes on the train ride back to New Jersey every night, so I could be as ready as possible when the performances began.

In addition, each time we got to a new city, after being on the bus for up to fourteen hours some days, I did a full ballet barre warmup while the regular cast did soundcheck. Then I'd work through the show on stage while I had the chance. Since I was mostly offstage, I understood how that time on the stage was precious and a golden opportunity that I needed to take advantage of whenever I could. After all, anything can happen in show business and often does, so I knew I had to be as prepared as I could be.

> *Having the capacity to anticipate obstacles in any business*
> *is a paramount skill to possess.*

During the show each night, if I was not covering anyone, my job was to sing background vocals in a booth with the other swings, but I was always looking beyond just my job requirements. I was looking to exceed expectations—my own expectations.

So, during the downtime between singing, I was rehearsing the show in the wings, as close as I could get to the stage, so I could *feel* the energy from the stage, as if I were on it. I aimed to put myself in as much of the atmosphere in which I'd be performing as I could, as often as I could. When others saw me, maybe thinking I was a little crazy and saying things like, "Woah, girl, why are you working so hard?" they didn't know that in my head, I *was* in the show.

As I danced in a small space on the side of the stage, I pictured myself under the lights with my family and friends in the audience watching me for the first time; that way, I felt the butterflies in my stomach that I always felt during a show. Even when I made a mistake, I practiced continuing on as I would in an actual show. By working that way, I was prepared for a real performance because I was not just practicing; I was practicing perfectly.

The truth is, I was thrown onstage in the middle of a show more times than I could possibly count, so I was continually grateful for the way I had been practicing. I'd be told, "Renée, you're on for *Victoria* tonight," and I would jet to the dressing room with my fellow swings to become *Victoria, the white kitten.* They would help me get my hair in pin curls, while I put on the five pounds of makeup, then my costume, and then went to the hair department to get my wig on. It was like being shot out of a cannon. Before I had a moment to think, I was onstage with the cast dancing and sweating it out in "The Jellicle Ball"—an almost ten-minute heart-pumping number toward the end of Act One. In those situations, when I got launched into the fire, practicing perfectly paid off big time. This technique was paramount not only for me but for the entire cast. I needed to ensure I knew the role I was onstage for inside and out, so I wasn't running into anyone by being in the wrong spot. Our safety depended on me knowing that role.

At one point, we were in Mexico for seven weeks, sometimes performing three shows per day. Everyone got sick at one point or another, so the swings were in the show constantly, both planned and unplanned. There were occasions when I played two or three different roles in one day, and because I practiced perfectly, I was able to be the best possible team player I could be.

No matter what we want to accomplish, we have to put in the work (practice). We have to do the work in building a career, being in a significant relationship, saving money to buy a home, getting in shape, learning a new trade—the list goes on. The great part about this, though, is when you're doing something that makes you happy, it's not really work.

The journey becomes exciting when your goal is clear and strong in your heart and mind's eye. As we go into the last step of our journey to becoming master communicators, remember the drive and passion that caused you to pick up this book, and don't just practice, practice perfectly.

"We are what we repeatedly do.
Excellence, then, is not an act but a habit."
— Will Durant

The following practices are simple, small shifts that make a huge difference and you can implement *now*.

Initiating Conversation

If you happen to be an introvert, and the thought of making conversation with someone else makes you want to shrivel up in a corner, here is a practice for you: Find your wing person. We all need one from time to time; usually, those people are our closest friends, colleagues, or family members. Tell that person you need them to hold you to a challenge. The challenge is to make conversation with any person who is sitting or standing next to you when you're out somewhere. It could be at a coffee shop, laundromat, doctor's office, the DMV, a grocery store, restaurant, or anywhere. The place doesn't matter. What matters is the confidence you can gather to initiate a conversation. The job of the wing person is to support you and give you a push when the fear creeps in.

I suggest planning to go out on the weekend with a friend you feel comfortable with. Tell them right from the beginning that this outing is not just for fun but also to help you gain more courage. Once they agree, pick a bar, restaurant, or lounge you're familiar with. Let your wing person know the goal is for you to start a conversation within the first fifteen minutes. This way, they know how to hold you accountable. The conversation doesn't have to be with someone you are interested in romantically; it could be anyone. The exercise is simply about firing up a conversation with another person to get you into the groove of doing so.

Making conversation will be uncomfortable at first like any new habit is, but the more you do it, the easier it becomes. Instead of thinking of this practice as a chore, make it a game. Begin keeping track of how many people you talk to, and the next night, try to beat that.

When joy is infused into anything you do, success follows.

Trust me, after trying this a few times, you won't need your wing person anymore because starting conversations will become natural and even a joy for you.

> *"Joy is the ultimate creator."*
> — Gabrielle Bernstein

Pausing Social Media

A while back, I taught a few classes at Canyon Ranch, a beautiful wellness resort in Lenox, Massachusetts, so Michael and I got to enjoy a three-night stay there. When we checked in, we were happy to find the facilities encouraged limited cellphone use restricted to the rooms or specified areas of the grounds. On several of our trips, Michael has said, "Can we just enjoy the trip and not worry about posting pictures on social media?" So, once we heard about the limited cell phone use, we looked at each other and smiled because we knew that meant pausing social media, thus giving us the full reset we needed.

Here is some of what happened:

First, I felt completely peaceful. Without the mind-activating blue light staring back at me as I'm usually reading posts and looking at photos, my brain relaxed and my entire system settled down. The subtle internal feeling of angst went away because I didn't feel like I was supposed to be doing something else or be somewhere else.

Second, I was present. While I was teaching, I was completely tapped into the beautiful people in my class. When we walked around the grounds, I took in all of the elements of nature, and when I was talking to my husband over dinner, that conversation was the only one that mattered.

Third, I felt *free*. Any time I disengage from the world of social media, I feel so free and liberated and always ask myself why I don't disengage more often. Putting a pause on social media is so powerful that I actually feel like a new person when I practice it, so I strongly suggest trying it out. It can be for a few hours, a full day, or as much as you'd like. If this scares you, start small and try for thirty minutes. You may feel so good that you will want to add more of these breaks to your day, and if nothing else, this practice will make you aware of how often you are connected. You'll realize how much you tune into social media out of sheer habit or addiction, and you'll be able to choose differently when you wish. Below, jot down how long you will pause social media each day—and no, my friend, while you are asleep doesn't count.

Reflections Section: *Pausing Social Media*

- How long will you pause social media each day? Remember, you can start small, and add time each week.

_____

_____

Challenging the Fear

Many people are very afraid of verbal communication. I have watched the most confident and outspoken people struggle with looking someone else in the eye and saying what they felt. The thought of making small talk or discussing a question or issue with someone head on is purely terrifying for them. I cannot fully express how many times I've been told, "I'm just not a confrontational person," when I ask someone why they haven't said what they felt. Please listen to me here, and listen well:

Communication does not mean confrontation.

These are two completely different things, so if you're one of the people who confuses the two, please use this statement as an affirmation every day. Just because you speak to someone face to face does not mean you are being hostile or confrontational. I have no idea where this belief originated, so let's bring some light to the misconception. Sure, there are situations where communication *becomes* confrontational, but they are not one and the same. I really want us all to understand this because by believing they are the same, we deny ourselves wonderful opportunities to understand each other.

Unfortunately, avoiding verbal communication has become easy to do because of the other options available. Consequently, the verbal muscle isn't being flexed, so just like the plant that isn't watered, it withers away. Then, when we have to connect verbally, it seems scarier than it really is.

When you find yourself needing to have a talk with someone but fearing verbal communication, ask yourself, "What will happen if I *don't* challenge the fear?" I will help you with some answers. You will keep the situation lingering, wasting time and energy (and you already know what a high cost that is). You may make the situation worse, and above all, you subconsciously hinder your spirit by showing yourself that you back down in the face of adversity.

Nick Santonastasso, an incredible speaker who was born with a rare genetic disorder called "Hanhart Syndrome," which left him with no legs and one arm, made a statement that struck a chord deep within me: "Every time we don't follow through, we diminish the relationship with ourselves." Do you know that dreadful pit in your stomach from being disappointed in yourself because you let fear stop you from doing something you told yourself you would do? That feeling results from not challenging the fear, so remind yourself of this when you want to back down.

When someone has offended or wronged you in some way, but you're afraid to stand up for yourself, think about this:

Sometimes your job is to be the mirror for others,
reflecting back their actions and the results of their actions.

Standing up for yourself does not mean being aggressive or disrespectful, but it does require bringing consciousness through love and grace, even when the other party doesn't seem to deserve that love or grace. Here's an example: When I lived in California, I joined a gym right around the corner from where I resided. The first day at the gym I needed to find a spot to stretch after doing some cardio, so I parked myself in a little area with no one close by. As I lay on my back to begin stretching, I noticed a young mother walking toward me with her adorable little girl. I quickly realized I was in the walkway leading to the daycare, and as the mother walked around me, I said, "I'm so sorry. I just realized I'm in the way." She responded in a very short and snarky way with, "Yeah, you are." My first thought was, "Oh, there is no way this is going to set the tone for my time in California."

I was outright shocked that she responded as if she had asked me to move three times, and I had refused. In fact, the response was *so* unwarranted that I just couldn't let the encounter go by without addressing it. My instincts told me this woman didn't spend much time thinking about how her actions affected anyone else, and I needed to be a reflection for her. So, I waited outside the daycare until she came back out. When she did, I very sincerely said, "Excuse me, miss, but there was no need to be so rude."

She was taken completely off guard, mumbled something, turned, and bolted for the locker room—a response we can all understand, I'm sure. Feeling fear and running the other way. I relocated to another part of the gym, and five minutes later, as I lay on my back once again, I felt a shadow standing over me. *It was the woman!* She said, "I am so sorry. You're right. I shouldn't have been so rude." Well, don't you know, I popped up like a Pop Tart, turned to her, and said, "Thank you so much. I really appreciate that." When I saw the look on her face when she came back, I understood she was not used to looking into a mirror—a spiritual mirror, that is. By standing up to her, I acted as that mirror for her, thereby helping her step outside of herself to see how her actions affected someone else. In turn, she'll be able to bring more consciousness to her future interactions.

> *When you change your perspective of "standing up"*
> *from being about you to being about them, the fear subsides.*

Fear is just a bully that makes us believe we are powerless. Just like any bully, though, when we stand up to it by doing what we fear, the bully retreats, and we gain our power back. Well, my friend, the time has come to gain our communication power back by using these practices. Write below a situation when you have challenged your fear, and also one when you let yourself down by not following through.

Reflections Section: *Challenging the Fear*

- What is a situation when you challenged your fear? How did that feel?

_____

_____

_____

_____

- What is a situation when you let yourself down by not following through? How did that feel?

_____

_____

_____

_____

Picking the Head Up, While Putting the Phone Down

When you are out, *be out.* Make a promise to yourself to put the darn phone away while you are out in the world. Just recently, I caught myself in the middle of a digital fix. I was in the waiting room at my dentist's office for only about five minutes when I automatically reached for my phone, and put in my earbuds. I began listening in on a Clubhouse room, and when I looked up for a moment, two adorable little girls were giggling brightly while trying to get my attention by waving to me. I suddenly felt irritated with myself because there I was like a robot, not even noticing! I was being the person I'm writing about! Bottom line:

When we have our heads down in a phone,
we are missing the life right in front of us.

I will never forget being out to dinner with a dear friend of mine when next to us sat a family of five—mom, dad, one teenager, and two young children. From the time they sat down, to the time they left, no one spoke. This included during the meal. Why, you might ask? Because each of them had their heads down in a digital device. The parents and teen on their cellphones, and the two children on their video games. No connecting with one another, no affection, no laughing, no joy. Just the "Facebook Stare," as my husband calls it. Watching this family miss out on beautiful moments together made me so sad that it set my desire to write this book in motion.

So, this practice is great for everyone.

When you are out with your friends, your family, or by yourself, decide to give your fingers a rest from texting and scrolling. Stay present by engaging in conversations with those around you and really listen to what they have to say. In an online course I took taught by Jim Kwik, called "Super Brain," he explained how even just having a phone out on the table while eating a meal can cause anxiety to the other people there. Placing your phone out of sight while spending time with others makes it a lot easier to stay present.

A few years ago, a new restaurant opened in my neighborhood and I'm all about checking out the new spots. If I could have a side hustle, it would be as the woman who goes around tasting food for restaurants and cafés and then writes little blurbs about it—talk about getting paid to do what you love. Anyway, I decided to check out the new restaurant, and I brought my computer along so I could write as I ate pancakes.

As soon as I walked into the restaurant, I said, "Good morning" to the man behind the counter, and asked him for menu suggestions. He was the owner who gave me the menu rundown, and after some small talk, asked me what I did for a living as he looked at the computer in my hand. I said I was a Broadway performer and I was working on my first book, hence the computer. His eyes lit up, and he said, "Wow, that's so awesome. I love theatre and studied music at Berkeley. In fact, my friend and I wrote an entire musical while we were there. Maybe I can pick your brain about some things in the business?" I said, "Absolutely." All because I took part in a little chit-chat, instead of having my head down in my phone, I made a new acquaintance named Matthew. Now, when my mother and I go to his restaurant for breakfast, he always checks in on us and we'll talk about his music writing, my book progress, and life in general. This restaurant has become my new favorite breakfast spot because the food is so delicious, and the kindness expressed by the entire staff through talking with their customers reminds me to leave my phone in my purse and enjoy having my head up. In turn, I connect with the wonderful people who work there and am more present, making my breakfast so much more enjoyable.

We hear so much about "being present" from our spiritual teachers, so this statement has become somewhat cliché, causing it to be over-looked. Clichés, though, become clichés because their original source was so spot-on. Being present is where it's at, and when you think back to moments when you were fully present, you can remember the wonderful feeling.

"Feel the power of this moment and the fullness of being.
Feel your presence."
— Eckhart Tolle

Another great way to allow presence into your life is simply to look around. Wherever you are, take notice of your surroundings—the sights, sounds, and smells. Feel your butt in the chair and your feet on the ground. Once you start doing this, you'll realize how much you actually miss every day because any spare moment is spent with your head down, shoulders hunched over, and mind focused on what's behind that little screen you're holding. You can start small, trying for only a few minutes as you begin the exercise. Then work your way up from there to maybe twenty minutes. You may be pleasantly surprised by how wonderful you feel. I've had some of the best times when I was living *in* the world through presence, rather than *outside* the world through the lens of digital technology.

Below, write down the moments of pure presence in your life—make sure you describe the feelings as vividly as you can. As you're writing each example, take a second to breathe deeply and put yourself back in that place so you can feel those feelings all over again. By doing so, you will attract more of that presence into your daily life.

Reflections Section: *Picking the Head Up, While Putting the Phone Down*

- When was a time you connected with someone because you had your head up, your phone down, and now they're in your life in some capacity?

_____

_____

_____

_____

- What are two moments of pure presence that you've experienced? Describe the feelings as vividly as you can. Take your time, and really put yourself back in those moments as you breathe deeply.

_____

_____

_____

_____

Tuning Into Your Pet

Do you have a pet you love more than anything in the world? If you do, you know how much joy these little lovebugs add to our lives and how they deserve our undivided attention. If you have a dog, like me, you also understand the strife sometimes of needing to walk your fur baby while still taking care of so many other errands. In my case, this often leads to carrying my phone with me as I walk Frank the Tank—my English Bulldog. One day, when I lived in California, I was walking Franky around our neighborhood and brought my phone along to check email as we walked. He went to the bathroom and I went to pick up after him when I realized I had no pocket to put my phone in. While I frantically looked around to find a place to put my phone, I must've looked like a whack-a-doo. I clumsily stuck the phone under my arm, while pulling out the bag to clean up his business. At that moment, I felt utterly embarrassed because I recognized I couldn't even go on a ten-minute walk without my phone. I was not able to give 100 percent of my attention to my beautiful dog, who is nothing but 100 percent attentive to me. To boot, I wasn't even appreciating the perfect view of the clear sky or the gorgeous landscape because I was too busy looking at a screen.

After that day, I decided to leave my phone inside the house when I walk Frank the Tank and my walks are so much more enjoyable now. Also,

I'm able to ensure he isn't doing anything mischievous because he knows I'm paying attention.

No matter what pet you may have, when you are with them, *be* with them. You may think giving them your full attention doesn't matter, but it definitely does. Don't you feel the difference when someone is giving you their full attention versus when they are half-listening? Your pet feels that difference too, so choose to make this small change and all involved will feel the happiness.

Turning Up the Kindness

Have you ever been in a huge rush, with your mind spinning, when someone holds the door open for you and smiles as you walk into a store, restaurant, or some other place? You stop in your tracks and snap back to reality as you realize that person's kindness? Instances like this are such a blessing because they're little reminders for us to slow down and take in the present moment. This brings me to my next practice, which is simply to get out of your own bubble by performing acts of kindness. Acts of kindness are so wonderful because they not only make the other person feel great, but they make you feel great for doing them.

Old-fashioned manners like holding doors open, helping someone with their bags, or saying "Hello," "Please," and "Thank you" can go a long way. But sometimes, those manners are lost in the landscape of new school technology.

The truth is, the person you hold the door open for may be struggling mentally and wrapped up in some deep negative thoughts. You have the ability through your gesture to change the path of their thought from "I feel invisible," to "Maybe there are good people in this world."

A powerful quote by Wendy Mass that I always refer to because of its amazing truth is: "Be kind, for everyone you meet is fighting a battle you know nothing about." Therefore:

> *When you practice acts of kindness,*
> *you can change the trajectory of a person's life.*

We never truly know the difference we make in each other's lives. Why not aim to make a positive difference while also learning to communicate better through small initiations like, "How is your day going?"

This practice involves bringing back manners not only as a means of communicating with others, but more importantly, because great manners make everyone feel great.

The practice goes like this: When you enter or leave someplace, put your phone away. Even if it's a super-important email you have to answer, wait until you are settled somewhere to do so. Get into the habit of breathing and holding the door open for the person before or after you. Say hello to the person next to you in line, and this one is my favorite:

When you notice something you like on or about someone, tell them!

If you like the color of their shirt or you love their smile, tell them. The best feeling is when I compliment a complete stranger and their face goes from lost in thought to happily surprised. What I often observe is that their body subtly shifts into a more open position, as if the compliment gave them the little boost of confidence they didn't know they needed.

When I was on Broadway, walking out the stage door after performing was a thrill that was never lost on me. I loved seeing the excited faces of the fans waiting to meet the actors, and when I signed a playbill for someone, I always made conversation because connecting with the fans was one of my favorite parts of being an actor.

One night after a performance of *Pretty Woman,* I met a woman who was smiling from ear to ear when I walked out the stage door. I went right up to her to say hello and sign her playbill. We began talking, and she told me she had been battling breast cancer for many years. After she shared her story with me, I said, "If you can find a way to stay in joy as often as you can, that is the best thing you can do for your health." She responded, "Between seeing this show today and you stopping to talk to me, I have felt more joy today than I have in a very long time!"

I have tears in my eyes just thinking about that moment because such moments confirm the power of kindness. By taking five extra minutes out of my night to say hello and have a brief conversation, I was able to bring a smile to someone's face and joy to their heart, which brought me joy too. How amazing is that? To see that woman happy made me happy, and I headed home that night feeling completely fulfilled.

Do you see what I mean? A little kindness goes a long way, and no matter how advanced technology becomes, the love and joy that human interaction brings can never be replaced. Now, grab yourself a cup of coffee or tea and settle in for a few minutes with the questions below. I'd like you to really look back at your life and tune into moments of kindness others provided and times when you showed kindness. Be specific about the situations and the feelings they conjured up. Answering these questions will be powerful for you because by taking the time to focus on those situations, you put yourself back into those elevated feelings, which is healthy for your mind, body, and soul. This will inspire you to practice more kindness inviting more of those good feelings into your existence.

Reflections Section: *Turning Up the Kindness*

- Describe two moments of kindness initiated by someone else. How did they make you feel?

_____

_____

_____

_____

- Describe two moments when you practiced acts of kindness. How did the person react? How did you feel?

_____

_____

_____

_____

_____

Chapter Eight

STEPPING INTO YOUR POWER
(PRACTICES PART 2)

*"Take advantage of every opportunity to practice your
communication skills so that when important occasions arise, you
will have the gift, the style, the sharpness, the clarity,
and the emotions to affect other people."*
— Jim Rohn

How often do you have something serious to address with someone and you get that accomplished without an actual conversation? We've all tried the long text threads and emails that go on and on, but without that face-to-face contact, it's beyond difficult to truly understand the significance of the situation. As we have learned, if you cannot communicate in person, a video call is the next best thing because you can see the person and their body language as you talk, and they can see yours. These factors create a much higher level of communication than just typed words.

Real Talk

> *"Because no matter how hard a conversation is, I know that on*
> *the other side of that difficult conversation lies peace.*
> *Knowledge. An answer delivered. Character is revealed.*
> *Truces are formed. Misunderstandings are resolved. Freedom*
> *lies across the field of the difficult conversation. And the*
> *more difficult the conversation, the greater the freedom."*
> — Shonda Rhimes

As someone who has been in her fair share of predicaments because of typed words being misconstrued, trust me when I say that when there is something pertinent to discuss, it's best to have a real, spoken conversation.

A few years back, I had a misunderstanding with a dear friend over text. I knew the situation could easily escalate if not dealt with right away, so I picked up the phone. My friend decided not to answer, and instead, kept texting for hours upon hours. Nothing was resolved, and the situation got worse because without hearing the tone of my voice or feeling my genuine energy, there was a whole lot of assuming. This, of course, added to the frustration on both ends, and instead of bringing us closer, pushed us farther apart.

When we attempt to resolve pressing matters through texts
or email, we are like two people talking through a brick wall
and trying to hear one another.

I cannot fully express how deeply upsetting this situation was for me. What started out as a misunderstanding grew into a knock-down, drag-out word battle, wasting time and breaking hearts—the sad and preventable result of a refusal to talk. The part that bothered me the most was I *knew* we could resolve the issue in five minutes if we *just had a conversation.* Instead, the issue lingered on for years, until we finally ran into each other.

When we did, she tried to ignore me at first, until I apologized and explained that I hadn't wanted any of this to happen, which is why I had called her to speak on the phone several times. Her guard immediately went down, and I could tell she recognized how unnecessary the misunderstanding had been.

We've moved forward since then, but these kinds of situations happen all the time. Family and friends don't speak for decades, and when they finally do, they don't even remember why they were upset. Isn't that so sad? Years that could have been spent enjoying life together, and making great memories were used up by what I call:

"Assumption animosity"
—animosity felt from what one assumes to be true.

Make a pledge to yourself here and now that when there is even the slightest hint of tension or the possibility of a misunderstanding rising over text or email, you will pick up the phone, have a video call, or meet in person to have a *real talk*. Save yourself the stress you'll encounter by not doing so.

Reflections Section: *Real Talk*

- Write down a time when you were involved in a misunderstanding and avoided a "real talk." What were the consequences?

- Write down a time when you were involved in a misunderstanding and engaged in a "real talk." What were the consequences?

_____

_____

_____

_____

Writing a Letter

Have you ever felt really touched by a card or a letter you received from someone? You read the heartfelt message, with the individual touch of the written words, and it brought tears to your eyes, or laughter or joy to your heart? Well, this practice is dedicated to offering someone else the experience of being touched by your written words to evoke uplifting emotions. So, the practice works like this: Once a month, sit down with a pen and a piece of paper and think of someone who has inspired you in some way. It could be someone currently in your life, or someone you haven't been in touch with for years (which makes this even more fun). The letter can be as long or as short as you choose, but write from the heart.

If you don't usually feel comfortable doing that, *great!* That feeling of uneasiness means you are breaking through your communication barrier. So, when that feeling shows up, celebrate it, and let that push you to keep going. Keep tapping into your heart and continue writing from there.

Once you are finished and have read the letter over, don't spend too much time analyzing what you've written. Too often, we mull over our words, which lets our fear kick in and drive us crazy as we second-guess everything we've written. Set a timer, giving yourself about twenty minutes to fix some things, if need be. When the timer is up, make yourself put the letter in an envelope, address it, stamp it, and send it off.

This practice is one of my favorites because not only am I a sucker for a good ol' school handwritten letter (as you already know), but it's a two-for-one gift. When you write a letter, you have the capacity to make someone's day a bit brighter through your words, while you grow to become more comfortable expressing your feelings on paper. How awesome is that?

Reflections Section: *Writing a Letter*

- Recall a time when you wrote someone a handwritten letter. How did the person react? How did you feel doing it?

_____

_____

_____

_____

- Recall a time when you received a handwritten letter. How did you feel after receiving it?

_____

_____

_____

_____

Texting with Intention

This practice is all about intentional texting. Here's how it works: When you think of someone out of the blue who you haven't spoken to, but would love to, send them a text saying, "Hey, I was just thinking about you. How are you?" When you text them this easy-going yet honest question, it is a way of beginning a conversation, showing them you care, and also getting past an ego game—*not wanting to be the first one to engage.*

Have you ever experienced the following situation? You want to reach out to someone, but you haven't spoken to them, so you go into the "Three Act Play" over why they haven't reached out to you first, and your assumptions make you decide to wait until they contact you. "Well, I'd love to catch up with him, but he's always so busy, so why should I be the one to reach out? He'll get in touch when he's ready." Why do we turn reaching out into a game? No matter what the scenario is, if someone's on your mind, don't overanalyze; just contact them. We let our egos take the lead, and the next thing we know, we haven't talked to someone important in our lives in several years. I understand this because I have played this ego game myself.

I've thought of some great memories with a friend I haven't spoken to for a while, but since I was the last one to reach out, I held off from doing so again because I thought, "Well, I don't want to be a bother. If they were interested in talking, they'd contact me." I failed to realize that the person on the other end could have had a lot on their plate, and even though they wanted to catch up with me, maybe a casual chat wasn't first on their priority list. The second agreement in Don Miguel Ruiz's book *The Four Agreements* is "Don't take anything personally." The quicker we learn not to take anything personally, the better off we'll be, and here is a great reminder to help us refrain from doing so:

We are not the center of everyone's universe.

I know this realization can be a tough pill to swallow, but once we realize it, it serves us immensely.

Others have a million things going on in their lives just like you. Instead of feeling slighted, "Be the change."

If you think of them, text them *no matter who was the last to engage.* This practice is that easy. Trust me, when I do this, the result is always positive. Often, I'll get a text back that says, "I'm so happy you reached out," or "I've been thinking about you too, how weird!" Then we find a time to actually talk, and we are reconnected. If that person doesn't respond, that's okay too, because by reaching out to them, you're at least letting them know where you stand!

Reflections Section: *Texting with Intention*

- Have you ever played the ego game of not wanting to be the first to engage? If so, what did you tell yourself that stopped you from reaching out?

_____

_____

_____

_____

- How did it turn out by not reaching out?

_____

_____

_____

_____

- Can you recall a time you texted someone out of the blue and something good came out of it? Explain.

_____

_____

_____

_____

Just Say No

As a child growing up in the '90s, I was inundated with the phrase, "Just say no," which was part of an advertising campaign for a program called Drug Abuse Resistance Education (D.A.R.E.). This short phrase was meant to give children a simple answer, sending them in the right direction when faced with drugs. As an adult, this phrase has come to mean so much more for me.

Every day we have our to-do lists, and if we're lucky, we get at least a few of those things done. Often, other things we didn't anticipate arise and need our attention, so our to-dos go toodle-loo. Such is life, right? Now, if you have what I call the "PPP" (people-pleasing pattern), you're even more lucky to get any of your priorities accomplished because you're too busy saying yes to everyone else's.

Here is where "Just say no" comes in handy. As a woman with the PPP myself, I understand how the idea of "Just say no" can be quite difficult to grasp, but to be your most authentic self, you need to try. If you often agree to take part in things you don't really want to be a part of, or you take on more than you can handle because you feel guilty, then listen up, my dear one.

When "OPP" (other's people's problems) take priority over your own because you fear disappointment and guilt, then you have the PPP.

The people-pleasing pattern is very tricky because it gives you a sense of satisfaction and dissatisfaction at the same time. You feel satisfied because you're being of service to others and dissatisfied because you've done so at the cost of your own needs.

Every time we say yes when our gut is telling us no, we are being dishonest with ourselves and others.

This book is about getting us back to our truest selves through authentic communication, so that means we must kick the PPP to the curb.

True communication equals honesty, and we can only be honest with someone else when we've first been honest with ourselves.

This realization is imperative to learning how to "Just say no." To put this phrase into practice, the next time someone asks something of you, I'd like you to take five minutes before answering. If you're on the phone and that means you have to call back, then do so. If you're face-to-face and it means saying, "Hold that thought. I have to run to the bathroom," then do that to check in with yourself. I know from experience that when you have the PPP, your first reaction is yes and it happens before you even have time to think about it. By taking five minutes to breathe and tune into your body, you give your mind a chance to tap into what your gut truly wants. If your gut is telling you no, then do not allow the mind to convince you otherwise. Go back to the person and speak from the heart. Say something along the lines of, "Because I care about you, I need to be really honest. I would love to be able to help you, but I can't right now because I have so much on my plate, and I'm feeling completely overwhelmed!"

Yes, my PPP people, this will definitely feel uncomfortable at first because you are not used to saying no. It might even feel weird the first ten times you say no because you are breaking a pattern, and as with any pattern-breaking, it's uncomfortable. I will tell you this, though. That discomfort is much better than the resentment you'll feel by continually putting your needs second. The other person may be upset or disappointed, but that will pass because, at the end of the day, they cannot fault you for being upfront.

By saying no, you will have courageously faced your fear of disappointing others by staying true to yourself and being honest with the other person. There is no stronger communication than that. When you "Just say no," you are gifting yourself with a form of self-care, and here is a truth for you:

Self-care is not self-ish.

Having the heart to serve is one of the most beautiful qualities to possess, but we must not get caught up in the belief that service means sacrificing our wellbeing. Let's flip the script and start believing that taking care of ourselves allows for *more* service to others. When you are overly tired from not getting sleep for a few nights, how patient do you feel with your children? When you are overworked from covering for a coworker's vacation for two weeks, how loving are you to your spouse when you get home at night? When you take care of yourself, you are better equipped to take care of others, and I cannot think of anything that is further from selfish; can you?

I'd like to address another part of this whole "Just say no" thing. When someone invites you somewhere and you don't want to go, or if someone asks if you'd be interested in doing something and you're not, please *Just say no.* I don't know about you, but nothing is worse for me than when you're the one trying to plan an event and people don't respond to you one way or the other, so you're left hanging in limbo. I'm going to shoot it to you straight here—that is *rude*!

Please take three seconds to respond via spoken word, text, or email, and say, "I can't attend, but thank you," or "Thanks, but I'm busy," or "Can't make it." I realize some people believe no response *is* a response, but that is plain false. If someone is taking the time to ask, please be respectful and respond. We are better than that, people, so let's hold ourselves accountable and "Just say no!"

Below, list examples of when you said yes to something when you needed to say no. Examples are going out to dinner with friends when you didn't have the money so you wouldn't disappoint them, doing your child's science project because they were crying about it being too hard, or telling a coworker you would help them with their presentation when you were struggling to complete your own.

The situations are endless, and once you start thinking back and listing them, your eyes will be opened to how often you people please.

Also write down a time you didn't respond to someone's invite because you wouldn't be attending what they invited you to. Then, write down a time when others didn't respond to you.

Reflections Section: *Just Say No*

- List two examples of the PPP making you say yes when your gut told you no. How did you feel doing those things? Be specific about the feelings. (Examples: I felt resentful. I felt stressed out. I felt angry.)

_____

_____

_____

_____

- List one time when you didn't respond to someone because you would not be attending what they invited you to. Looking back, could have you taken the time to "Just say no"?

_____

_____

_____

_____

- List one time when you were left hanging because others didn't respond to your invitation. How did you feel?

_____

_____

_____

Journaling Through Video

This practice is *so much fun*! As we discussed in Chapter Six, video calls are becoming the new normal, but many people are still uneasy with this way of connecting. When I initially work with clients to help them with connecting on camera, they usually struggle the most with talking to a screen. This makes total sense because when you really think about it, you're talking to a screen. A screen. Yes, there is a person on the other side, but it is through the medium of a screen. That can feel so weird. This practice is meant to help you find ease with bringing your most genuine self to video.

So, how do we do this? Well, we use the camera as we would a written journal, which you know I am big on. In a journal, you release the thoughts stored in your subconscious through your hand and onto the page. The only difference here is you use spoken words and a camera. This can seem quite intimidating, but it may make you feel better to know that *no one hears this but you*. This practice is specifically for you to get comfortable bringing your real self to video and not shying away the minute the camera goes on.

I recommend using your phone's camera for video journaling because you can then do it anywhere, but feel free to use your computer as well. All you have to do is press record on the camera and talk. Talk about your day, the weather, how you're frustrated with work, or whatever comes through.

Feel free to put the camera down somewhere like a windowsill so you can talk while doing other things. You can do your laundry, wash the dishes, make your bed, or just stand there if you wish. What you're doing does not matter. All that matters is that you express your thoughts vocally while the camera is on. This practice does a couple of things:

1. It gets you familiar with the feeling of talking while the camera is on. (Trust me; soon you won't even feel the difference between talking on video and talking in person.)
2. It gives you a release by talking out things you may have been keeping inside, just like when you use a written journal.

Really let yourself be free when doing this because talking about what's on your mind takes those things out of your mind, giving you an emotional release. The best part is you can erase the video immediately. How great is that? It's equivalent to writing down your fears on a piece of paper and burning the paper afterward.

As I said, start small. At first, just talk about trivial things, and then, when you get more comfortable, you can speak to the camera like it's your therapist. Go wild! Let the questions arise and the tears flow. Before you know it, you will love video journaling, and feel at ease in front of the camera for video calls and virtual meetings.

Do yourself a favor—try this now. I know what you're thinking. "Renée, I'm not even finished reading this chapter." I realize that, but there is a method to my madness. By jumping into this now, before you're ready, you prove to yourself that you can *do* it despite the *fear*. So, go right now. It can be thirty seconds, but *do it*! When you're done, write down below how you felt doing this practice for the first time. I am so excited for you, my friend. I have chills right now because I know this exercise will help you greatly.

Reflections Section: *Journaling Through Video*

- How did you feel when talking to the camera like a virtual journal? What thoughts, feelings or questions arose?

_____

_____

_____

_____

Alone Time

I find this last exercise to be the most beneficial in bringing yourself into alignment—mind, body and spirit. Every single day, we are bombarded with diversions from various mediums that take us far away from our-selves—our inner selves, the basis of our beings, the root of everything else. Now more than ever, our quiet time is extremely precious because the majority of our lives are spent linked to the acceleration of the out-side world through technology. We constantly react to everything going on around us. The news, social media posts, several different conversations on Marco Polo, Clubhouse, email, texts, the newest ways to stream tele-vision, the latest video games, operating system updates every few weeks, and the list goes on.

With all this, the moments left for us to power down and be still become few and far between. Then we wonder why we often feel agitated and like our minds are all over the place. It's because they *are* all over the place. To get back to our most authentic selves, we have to make quiet time a must, and the quickest way to do this is through meditation. Many people get a little nervous when you mention the word *meditate* because they think meditation requires clearing the mind of all thoughts. I, too, was one of those people until I began studying Transcendental Meditation. No matter what kind of meditation you try, the goal is to become an observer of the thoughts in your mind because, in actuality, you are the one behind the thoughts. Notice that I said "*the* thoughts" and not "*your* thoughts." That's because most thoughts are not *yours*. They are universal thoughts you have, I have, and we all have. They are often based in fear because our brains are conditioned to protect us from danger, so they are always looking for what's wrong.

> *"What a liberation to realize that the*
> *'voice in my head' is not who I am."*
> — Eckhart Tolle

Meditation is for observing the endless stream of thoughts that go through our minds second to second, as opposed to being a participant in those thoughts. When we participate in the thoughts, we jump on the rollercoaster of emotions that come with those thoughts, sending our minds and bodies into a frenzy.

Meditation is a beautiful practice that allows our system to take a break and detach from the rest of the world by closing our eyes and focusing within. Our breath is our life force, and by centering in on that breath, we slowly reset our minds and bodies. Through meditation, we are able to watch the thoughts arising like ocean waves crashing on the shore. We can then find our stillness like the deep water below the ocean's surface.

If meditation is unfamiliar to you, start slowly—five minutes a day. Sit in a quiet space, set an alarm, close your eyes, and as the thoughts arise, watch them. Watch how active and erratic the mind is, and allow those thoughts to be there as you just breathe. Focus on your breath moving in and out. Trust me, the more you do this, the more you learn to detach from those thoughts and understand that you are not the thoughts but an observer of them.

Before you have a chance to get busy, start your five-minute meditation after you finish this chapter. Don't be surprised by the feelings that may show up because sometimes when we stop and tune into our inner life, the emotions we've kept buried appear. Anxiety, confusion, happiness, sadness, joy, elation, anger, and anything else can pop up. Write the emotions down in the Reflections Section after your five minutes are up. As you make meditation a new practice, I recommend you continue to write down the emotions that show up in each of your meditations in your journal. By documenting them, you can get more acquainted with your inner self through visually seeing what you feel on paper. This will shine some light on patterns you notice and facilitate moments of clarity for you.

To add to this last practice of alone time, try practicing in nature because nature can be one of our greatest teachers. The water in the ocean doesn't try to create waves, just like trees don't try to grow, so these elements of nature serve as reminders that living things are effortless. I don't know about you, but anytime I'm next to the ocean, I feel a sense of unbounded serenity and wholeness.

Nature simply is. If we can realize that we as humans simply are, we can walk throughout our lives much more peacefully.

Your heart doesn't try to beat, and your lungs don't try to breathe. They just do so without your even thinking about it. Connecting to nature is a wonderful way to slow yourself down and recharge. Sit in the grass of a park among the trees, lie on a beach while digging your toes into the sand, hike up a mountain, or simply stand outside and surrender to the wind caressing your skin. Open your eyes; take nice deep, belly breaths, and observe everything around you. Take a journal in case you feel inspired to write about your experience or anything you may feel. No matter what part of nature you choose, declare that once a week you will take at least one hour to unplug and be in nature. By staying present in nature, you begin to align with your truest self. Sounds pretty good, huh?

Reflections Section: *Alone Time*

- What came to mind while you meditated for five minutes?

_____

_____

_____

_____

- Were you able to observe your thoughts and not be *in* them? If so, what was that like?

_____

_____

_____

_____

_____

- How did you feel after the five minutes were up?

_____

_____

_____

_____

- Do you declare to be in nature for one hour a week?

_____

_____

_____

_____

_____

Chapter Nine:

SEIZING AN OPPORTUNITY

"Sometimes, if you want to see a change for the better,
you have to take things into your own hands."
— Clint Eastwood

In the winter of 2013, I began playing the role of Mary Delgado in *Jersey Boys* on Broadway. I lived right on 52nd Street between Eighth and Ninth Avenues, five minutes down the street from the August Wilson Theatre where the show was playing. The role was a dream come to life for me. As a true Italian Jersey girl who grew up listening to Frankie Valli and The Four Seasons, *Jersey Boys* hits close to home both literally and figuratively. I was born and raised just a few miles from where the entire storyline takes place, and I understood the essence of Mary Delgado—the strong and sassy spitfire who became Frankie Valli's first wife—very well. In the acting world, we call it "type casting," and my "type" was a perfect match for Mary Delgado.

I was incredibly fulfilled that year. I was in love with the man I was dating, living in New York City in a beautiful apartment where I could stand on my front steps and see the marquee of the Broadway show I was in, and doing what I loved for a living—performing eight shows a week in one of the greatest musicals of all time. I did not take one second of any of it for granted.

I had previously been a universal swing for three different companies of *Jersey Boys*, for six months, which meant I covered all three female roles in the Las Vegas production, the Chicago production and the first national tour. During those months, I would fly back and forth from Vegas, to Chicago, and to wherever the tour was located at that point in time. Although the overall show was the same, there were slight variances with each company, so I had three different sets of index cards and notes for each production. That way, I was fully prepared to step into any of the female roles for all three companies. After those six, very exciting months, I moved into the role of Mary Delgado for one year on the first national tour.

Being on the road with the show was incredible, but there was nothing like being on the Great White Way! My family and friends could drive right through the Lincoln Tunnel to come see me in a musical about where we come from, and they did just that.

A few months into my run with the show, we started hearing that casting was beginning for the *Jersey Boys* movie. The world of Broadway is a small and tight-knit community, so any news travels fast.

To be honest, I didn't think much about the film because I figured they would be hiring A-list celebrities for the roles out of Los Angeles, so I continued with my eight shows a week, loving each and every moment. Then during one Sunday matinee, I was backstage when a fellow cast member said Clint Eastwood was in the audience. Eastwood was going to be directing the film, so he was watching all of the different productions of the show to see how the actors played the roles.

I will never forget walking out on stage for "My Boyfriend's Back." When I turned to face the audience, ten rows back, staring right at me, was the legend himself, Clint Eastwood! Well, the show went great that day, and we all met and took a photo with Mr. Eastwood afterward. A few weeks later, members of our cast began getting calls to audition for the film. At that point, I thought, *Well, it would be pretty awesome to be a part of the film, even if I was just a face in a crowd scene.*

When I called my agent to ask about getting an audition appointment, she said, "I'm on it." A couple of weeks passed, and then the casting department for the film put out a breakdown (a description of the type of person they are seeking) for the role of Mary Delgado. In other words, they still hadn't cast someone for Mary. I could not believe they had not found someone yet for the movie's female lead. So, I called my agent once again, this time to have her contact casting about me auditioning for the role of Mary, and again she said, "I'm on it."

I went about my business as usual, and as the days went on, several women I knew got appointments for the role of Mary. I waited patiently, wondering why I hadn't been called. I mean, I knew I was the right type for the role because I was currently playing Mary at the highest level someone could be playing her—on Broadway, so I thought that at least warranted an audition, right?

Finally, my agent called and said, "Renée, I don't know what the problem is. I tried and tried, but they won't give you an appointment for Mary, but they offered you one for an Angel who sings, 'My Boyfriend's Back.'"

I thought, *Wait, what?* How could they not see me for the role, yet they were seeing several other women who had never played the role, and who weren't the type described in the breakdown? I was genuinely confused, and after about forty-five minutes of feeling sad and disappointed, I vividly remember sitting on my couch, physically throwing my hands up, and saying, "What am I gonna do? I did everything I could, so I'm going to go in and audition for an Angel!"

We all face those times when we are trying and trying, but no matter what we do, the situation does not seem to change. At such times, we have two options: We can keep beating our heads against the wall, staying in the feelings of anger, frustration, and sadness, asking why, or we can take the second option. This option is the one I know to be much more beneficial. We physically and spiritually throw our hands up, fully surrendering, and trusting that what is meant for us will not miss us. Gabrielle Bernstein says in her book *The Judgment Detox*, "There is nothing more powerful than releasing the need to control and relying on a power greater than you to restore your thoughts and energy."

The morning of the *Jersey Boys* audition, I had another audition in Midtown Manhattan first. It was a rainy day, so after the first audition, I put my hair back in pin curls to travel from Midtown to Downtown Wall Street amid the downpour. Yes, this is the life of an actor. Always traveling with a Mary Poppins bag full of everything and anything needed to transform yourself into the next character.

Before the audition, the casting director, Geoffrey, and I had a great conversation. He told me he had seen the show the previous night and loved it even more than the first time he saw it. I explained I was really from New Jersey and lived right next to where the whole story takes place. After our casual chat, Geoffrey asked if I wanted to sing the song for my Angel audition first or read the scene. Before I answered, I took a deep breath, and my gut instinct came forward as a quiet, little voice that said, *You have to do this—it feels too right.* My brain didn't even have a chance to intervene.

I looked the casting director right in the eyes and said, "I have to be honest with you, Geoff. I was really hoping to come in and read for the role of Mary Delgado."

The words came from the deepest part of my soul, as if spirit were speaking through me. I had no idea how Geoffrey would react, but what I did know was that the truest part of me had stepped up to make sure I was true to myself. If I wanted to live without regret, I had to say what I felt.

The quiet voice is the voice of your soul.

He looked right back at me with kind eyes and a sense of ease, and said, "I was just thinking the same thing."

I nearly fell off the chair because I was so happily stunned. He then told me I could sing and read the scene for the Angel first, and that I could come back another day for the Mary scenes if I needed more time to go through them. I swiftly responded, "Oh, thank you, but I'll do it today!" (I sure as heck wasn't leaving that building until I did the audition I worked so hard to get!)

So, I did the Angel audition, and then Geoffrey gave me some time to go into the hallway and look over the material for Mary. The Mary audition consisted of two different scenes, which I performed a couple of times with Geoffrey. The audition went very well, and I left that day feeling elated.

I was elated simply because I got the chance *to* audition. If the *Jersey Boys* film came out and I never had the option to read for a role—one I was playing eight times a week while they were holding auditions *for* that role—I would have been crushed.

Often, as an actor, when you finish an audition, you cannot stop analyzing everything about that audition. How you looked, how you sounded, the casting director's reaction, etc. You can spend hours, days, even weeks stressing about it, waiting for a callback, or waiting to hear if you booked the job.

With my Mary audition, I didn't encounter that stress because my focus wasn't on getting the job. My focus was on being given a chance. Therefore, after the audition, I was able to be present in the bliss I felt. Through hearing and following what my gut was telling me in that room, I was able to effortlessly verbalize my desire to the casting director, and the Universe supported me fully.

By listening to your gut, you are communicating with your spirit, and spirit is where the truth lies.

This moment made me realize that when you follow your gut instincts, you cannot go wrong. By speaking up, I took my career into my own hands and gained an opportunity. On my way back to the subway that day, I was floating down the street with joy. I passed by a church and felt the pull to walk inside. I lit a candle and kneeled to give thanks because I was filled with so much gratitude for what had just happened.

A few weeks later, I was at my parents' home in New Jersey with my mom, dad, and grandmother, about to leave for my brother's wedding. Five minutes before we walked out of the house, I looked down at my phone and realized I had a missed call from my agent. I walked into my childhood bedroom and called her back. She picked up but put me on hold right away. When she came back, I could tell I was on speaker. She was on with my other two agents when she said, "You're Mary Delgado in the movie. Clint Eastwood loved you!" I literally left my body for a second and immediately began screaming my head off in exhilaration.

I ran into the living room, where my parents and grandmother were, crying. My mother said, "What's wrong?" I said, "I'm gonna be in a movie!"

My dad cried, my mother was shocked, and my ninety-year-old grandmother teared up and said, "I've been praying for this for years." I was overcome with pure bliss because this achievement was beyond what I had ever dreamed.

Sometimes what we dream doesn't hold a candle to what we achieve.

Filming Time

> *"Leap, and the net will appear."*
> — John Burroughs

We began filming in August of 2013, and I was flown to Los Angeles, first class, for my very first time. Talk about giddiness. I was like, "Wow, so this is what luxury feels like." Michael, who was still my boyfriend at that point, was with me the entire time, but here's a fun fact for you. Before we found out that I had booked the film, he was planning to propose to me. He had taken my dad out to dinner to ask for his blessing, and he had gone over to my parents' house to show my mother and grandmother the ring, but once I found out about the film, he decided to wait until after I finished filming. He didn't want to take any of my focus away from the experience of my first movie. Talk about selfless, right? That's one of the many reasons I said yes when he proposed the day after my filming was complete and we flew back home.

I had to share that special story with you, but let's get back to the film. When we arrived in Los Angeles, I was so nervous to drive from the airport to our hotel, because as a New Yorker living in Midtown, I hadn't driven in a while. Michael, in true Michael fashion—consistently motivating me to stand in my power—said, "You got this, Renée. You know what you're doing." And sure enough, after a few days, driving in the LA sunshine became one of my favorite pastimes. Let's be honest; if you live in Los Angeles, you better get comfortable driving because the car becomes your second home.

When I received my shooting schedule, I decided once again to take my career into my own hands. I asked if I could come to the set a day early to meet everyone and get accustomed to the atmosphere. Filming a movie was a brand-new experience for me, and I was starting at the top with a major feature film, so I wanted to give myself every possible chance for success.

What I didn't want to do was show up on the first day completely over-whelmed because of the newness of the whole experience. Going in the day before, without the pressure of filming, I allowed myself to become a bit familiar with the world into which I was stepping. That day, I met several of the crew and got to sit in on one of the scenes, which was priceless. I also met all the hair and makeup team, who then decided that, since I was there, they could paint my nails ahead of time to be ready for the follow-ing day. Through the power of conversation with the wonderful hair and makeup team, I was able to get a head start on my new endeavor by asking questions about the filming process, how things were run on set, and learn-ing about their stories. If I didn't communicate from my heart the request to visit the set the day before my work began, I wouldn't have acquired the valuable information I did. I also wouldn't have gotten to know and connect with the team of people helping me to transform into my character, before having to jump right into business.

In truth, communicating from my heart has always proved the right path, which only confirms the power of authentic communication.

My first day of filming came, and I woke up feeling like it was Christmas morning, mixed with the pride of college graduation and the positive anticipation of something huge about to happen! I got picked up and taken to the Warner Brothers lot, where hair and makeup and my trailer were.

Yes, I had my own trailer—well, a quarter of a trailer, but you may not understand how big this was for me. As a Broadway gal, I was conditioned to share a five by seven dressing room with eight other women, so having my own space was a *big deal.* To add to the fun, I didn't have to do my own hair or makeup either!

And my all-time favorite part of being in a film—the catering. I couldn't believe when one of the production assistants asked me what I wanted for breakfast and how I liked my coffee. I was used to grabbing a pre-packaged dinner on the way to the theatre, so I was in heaven!

Once my hair and makeup were complete and my breakfast finished, I went back to my trailer to put on my beautiful Mary dress. I'll never forget taking my first photo in costume—through the mirror—and having my girlfriends share in the thrill with me when I sent them the photo.

Next, it was time to get shuttled to the location of my first scene—the initial meeting of Mary Delgado and Frankie Valli.

As I sat in the shuttle by myself, in the gorgeous dress, I realized what I was about to do. The butterflies in my stomach began to move swiftly, and I felt like I was about to jump off a cliff. Once again, I turned within and heard that quiet voice say, *You know what you're doing. Clint Eastwood hired you, so trust in your talent and leap.* Then, I looked up to where I believe God resides and said, "Okay, here we go."

When I stepped out of the shuttle, all I could hear was the second assistant director speaking into her walkie talkie saying, "Team A has arrived. Team A has arrived." The door opened to the building where we were shooting, and the second I entered, I immediately felt a warm energy engulf me as everyone on the crew lovingly said, "Renée, welcome!"

The next thing I knew, the man himself, Clint Eastwood, walked up to my right side and said, "You know, I went around to all the different casts, but nobody was in your class. Then you came in and put yourself on tape, and it was the icing on the cake."

I had to hold back my tears of gratitude because, number one, I couldn't ruin my professionally done makeup, and two, I still had my first scene to film. The moment was so surreal that I knew it would be one I'd never forget.

The time had come to put my self-trust into effect by stepping into the shoes of Ms. Mary Delgado, for my first time onscreen. As Frankie Valli sang onstage, I leaned back with my elbows on the bar, staring at John Lloyd Young—who played Frankie Valli—like a lioness about to pounce. In that moment, as the camera moved up to stare me right in the face, it was as if I locked into my power and felt totally grounded. The butterflies were still there, but they sat composed behind my focus.

In hindsight, I can see I was grounded because I let go and trusted. I trusted I was exactly where I was meant to be. As you can imagine, with each moment of this new experience, I was soaking in every little thing I could, like a fawn learning to walk.

To express how fresh this all was to me, let me offer you an example. We did one or two takes of that initial moment when Frankie and Mary lock eyes when we heard, "Cut. Let's take a break." I began talking with the incredible crew, with whom I quickly became friends, and when I looked over to where I was just standing for the scene, a woman, exactly my height and similar stature was standing in my spot. I could tell she was helping the camera crew with my placement for the shot and my first thought was, *Oh, wow, that is so sweet of her. We're on break, but I don't have a problem just standing there.*

Truth be told, I was used to tech days on Broadway, where I'd be sweating under the lights, standing in the same position in high heels for hours before getting a break. Hence, this break didn't feel warranted to me. Naively, I walked up to the woman and said, "Thank you so much, but I don't mind standing there." She seemed dismayed as I spoke to her, and a second later, the assistant director, Bernie, said, "Renée, you go and take your break and don't worry about this. This is her job."

She was the Mary Delgado stand-in! Her job was *literally* to stand in for me for technical purposes like camera set up and lighting before we actually filmed the scene. Here I was thinking *she* must have been thinking, *Wow, this woman is lazy. I might as well stand here because she isn't.* But really, she was just doing her job. Talk about learning as you go.

After we shot the scene, we went to lunch, and Eastwood and I ate together—something we ended up doing every time I was on set. As we sat and ate that first day, I said to him, "Clint, I have to tell you your team of people are just as wonderful and genuine as you are." He responded, "Life is too short to surround yourself with people who don't lift you up." I almost jumped out of my seat because that is a belief I share too, and I told him that.

I could not wait to get back to the hotel that night to share my magical day with Michael and my parents, whom I called back in New Jersey. I journaled every single detail of that day and every day that followed. I was not going to leave this amazing time to memory alone. I needed to document all of the specifics.

Each day on set, I was like a sponge. I would ask the Boss (as his team calls him) questions about everything from what the names of all the camera shots meant to how he started acting. One day, Eastwood even let me do something I told him I had always wanted to do. He let me *use the clapperboard* to announce one of the scenes and take numbers.

See, I could have easily just done my job, which was to play the role I was cast in, but I recognize the value of being a student at all times. I wanted to absorb every second of being in this new atmosphere and in the presence of one of the greatest actors, producers, and directors of all time.

Clint Eastwood taught me about so much more than just acting. He taught me about what matters most in life and what it means to be a remarkable leader.

He showed love and respect not from a pedestal, but as an equal, which shined through in his open communication with everyone on and off set, through simple conversations, and valuing his team's input.

Eastwood is a collaborator who does not operate from ego. That quality makes for a productive and pleasant work environment because it sets the standard for everyone who works for him and with him. Here is a powerful principle to remember for any leader:

The best leaders lead by being, not by telling.

As any member of a team, when your boss puts you in charge of a task or project, do you feel a sense of pride? Do you feel compelled to step up to the plate? Well, you may feel that way because that is your boss leading with trust. Their trusting you activates the trust in yourself and, in turn, gives you the confidence to carry out the task or project efficiently.

This was the case for me when Clint Eastwood gave John Lloyd Young and me free rein while filming a scene. The scene was Frankie, Mary, and their young daughter Francine sitting at the dinner table eating pasta and eggplant parmigiana. (As soon as they placed it in front of me, my eyes lit up, and I proceeded to tell everyone on set how eggplant is my favorite! Then, with each take, they'd put a new plate in front of me, and I felt like I was in heaven.) Okay, back to the actual scene. During the meal, Frankie is talking to Francine, and Mary is tipsy, making snide remarks to Frankie. After a couple of takes, Eastwood decided to let the camera keep rolling, while John and I improvised. (That means, we didn't say lines from the script, but we said what came to us in the moment.) For over five minutes, the two of us just exploded. There was yelling, there were emotions, and at one point, I even took the bread basket and threw it at him! When we were finished, there was silence on the set until one of the crew members yelled out, "Wow! That's just like my marriage." Everyone on set started laughing, and Eastwood walked up to us and said, "That was great; we got it."

As the three of us walked out together, he told us, "I can't wait to edit this one." One of the film editors told me how much Clint Eastwood did love editing that scene, and how it was one of the best. Unfortunately, as the saying goes, "It was left on the cutting room floor," and the scene was eliminated right before the final cut. That is show business, my friend. More significant than the scene making it into the film was Clint Eastwood placing his trust in us to deliver what he believed was possible in that scene. He didn't micromanage or make us feel incapable by telling us exactly how to say each line or what the intention had to be behind the words. He trusted us, which activated that trust within ourselves, giving us the confidence to feel free to let ourselves stay in the moment and develop the scene from there. As a result of leading us in that way, Eastwood received exactly what he needed from us as our director. John and I still talk about how special that day was for us on set.

Another special day was meeting Christopher Walken, who played Gyp DeCarlo, the mob boss, in the film. I was eating lunch with Eastwood when Walken sat down next to me. I introduced myself, and Eastwood explained that I was a part of the Broadway show. At that point, Mr. Walken asked me all about the Broadway show and how I enjoyed performing in the stage version. When he got up to leave, Eastwood said to me, "I think he's going to be good in this role, don't you?"

I giggled to myself, thinking about how unbelievable it was that an Oscar-winning director was asking me *my* thoughts about his casting choice of an Oscar-winning actor. I answered honestly and said, "Yes, he will be amazing in the role, and Clint, when you're filming, you have to say to him, 'I gotta have more cowbell!'" (It's a line from a famous *Saturday Night Live* skit with Christopher Walken, Will Ferrell, Jimmy Fallon, Chris Kattan, Chris Parnell, and Horatio Sanz. Check it out on YouTube.)

Eastwood laughed, and said, "Oh, *I will.*"

Well, my friends who played the Four Seasons reported back to me that the Boss did in fact say the line to Christopher Walken when they all finished filming the "sit down" scene. Eastwood said, "Hey, Chris, that was great, but we're going to do it one more time, and this time, I gotta have more cowbell." Clint Eastwood and everyone on set burst out laughing, while Christopher Walken just shook his head and walked away. Clint Eastwood is a man who sticks to his word—one of the many reasons he is a class act.

My entire film experience was a combination of moments that had me checking in with myself to make sure they were real. While sitting at dinner with Eastwood and the crew members one shoot day, after enjoying a piece of cake that closed out my meal, the actual Frankie Valli walked over to our table. I found myself sitting smack in the middle of these two superstars, and for a second, I left my body and looked down at myself from above, saying, "What is my life right now?"

I asked myself the same question the day that Clint Eastwood taught me one of the most impactful lessons of my life—the beauty of imperfection. We were on set filming the Frankie Vallie and Mary Delgado breakup scene. In the scene, tensions are high because Mary is drunk and expressing how sick and tired she is of Frankie not being around. After we did the first take, Eastwood said, "Okay, now I want you to really give it to him." So, in the second take, I completely unleashed when, all of a sudden, I forgot all my lines. I screamed in frustration, but then picked the lines back up a few seconds later. After the scene was finished, Eastwood said, "That was it." To which I responded, "But, Clint, I forgot my lines!"

He said, "It doesn't matter because it was raw, and it was real, and that's good. I used to tell that to Meryl when we were filming. I thought to myself, *Oh my goodness, Clint Eastwood is talking to me about Meryl Streep!* He continued on, "Meryl always liked to do several takes of her scenes until they were perfect, but when I began shooting her rehearsal takes, she realized how organic they were, and then she had me film them all the time." *This is unreal*, I thought. *The best of the best giving me advice through first-hand stories of another icon.* This is what you call "inspiration gold."

That was the beginning of me letting go of my perfectionism. Think about this. If I had kept to myself and only spoken when spoken to, all of those moments and lessons would not have happened, which is why becoming comfortable with communication outside of screens is so vital. We don't want to miss out on extraordinary opportunities.

The Moment of Truth

> *"Your gut is more powerful than anyone else's advice."*
> — Jamie Kern Lima

Weeks into the project, I was having lunch, once again, with the Boss and one of the producers of the film when they started talking about how Eastwood knew he wanted me for the role when he saw me on Broadway. When I heard this, I was so floored I actually stopped eating. (Let me remind you, he saw me perform on Broadway weeks and weeks before I got an appointment to audition. "So, then why was it a struggle to even *get* an appointment?" you ask. I wondered the same thing.)

I told them both, "Do you guys want to hear a funny story? I couldn't even get an appointment for the role of Mary, I only had one for an Angel." The producer asked, confused, "What do you mean? We specifically requested 'the girl from the Broadway company' to come in and audition." (Imagine my shock.) I said, "The only reason I got to audition for Mary is because I opened up my big mouth in the room, and asked Geoffrey if I could!"

Well, I came to find out that day that what had happened was a *miscommunication* with a casting associate who was juggling a few films at once and just dropped the ball. A miscommunication that could have cost me a life-changing opportunity if I had not verbally communicated my hope to audition for Mary Delgado.

Speaking up was the catalyst for a chain of events that made up one of the most magical experiences of my life.

If I hadn't spoken up for myself, another woman who looked similar to me and acted her butt off could have walked through the door and booked the job instead. Then I'd be sitting in the movie theater *watching Jersey Boys* instead of being on the screen *in Jersey Boys*. All the while, I'd be moving through life *never* knowing that Clint Eastwood was actually waiting for *me* to walk through that door! Playing Mary Delgado in the *Jersey Boys* film is one of the greatest honors of my life, and it all began with one moment of staying true to myself by listening to my intuition, and communicating from there.

If I let fear get in the way, as so many of us do when it comes to addressing things in our relationships, I could have missed a once-in-a-lifetime opportunity.

Every time I think about my *Jersey Boys* journey, I feel such deep emotion from the love, joy, and gratitude I have for the entire experience. I learned the most powerful lessons, acquired wonderful friendships, grew as a human being, and became proof that what's meant for you will not miss you.

Now that I've shared the ins and outs of my *Jersey Boys* story I want to highlight a few significant lessons for you to carry with you:

1. Just as I've explained, when a matter is crucial, a text message or an email won't cut it, and you must have a direct conversation. Well, the same goes for when someone else is working on your behalf. As hard as my agent worked to get me an audition appointment for the role of Mary through email and a couple of short conversations, I had to be the one to step up and have that direct interaction that left no space for miscommunication. This allowed me to shape my own destiny. Remember, at the end of the day, no one or nothing is a more precise representation of you than *you*.

2. Because I stay in constant communication with myself, on the day of the audition, I was able to tune into my gut, hear the quiet voice of my soul, and listen to it telling me to speak up for what I felt. Without my strong intrapersonal communication, the loud cries of my doubts and fears would have overshadowed that quiet voice, ultimately causing me to sit back and let an opportunity pass me by.

3. Remember when fear shows up in your life, ask yourself, "What happens if I *don't* face my fear?" Ruminating on the potential losses will give you a gentle nudge to take action in spite of the fear.

4. Knowing when to use authentic verbal communication can positively change the course of your life, and you deserve to seize every opportunity that comes your way by not letting a fear of speaking up hold you back. That alone is worth putting in the time to practice becoming a master communicator.

Reflections Section: *The Moment of Truth*

- Describe a time/times when you could have spoken up, but you didn't and missed an opportunity. How did you feel afterward?

_____

_____

_____

_____

- Describe a time/times when you listened to your gut, spoke up, and gained an opportunity or a relationship. What made you do that? How did you feel doing it?

_____

Chapter Ten:

CLAIMING WHO YOU WANT TO BE

"Our deepest fear is not that we are inadequate. Our deepest fear is that we are powerful beyond measure. It is our light, not our darkness that most frightens us. We ask ourselves, 'Who am I to be brilliant, gorgeous, talented, fabulous?' Actually, who are you not to be? You are a child of God. Your playing small does not serve the world. There is nothing enlightened about shrinking so that other people won't feel insecure around you. We are all meant to shine, as children do. We were born to make manifest the glory of God that is within us. It's not just in some of us; it's in everyone. And as we let our own light shine, we unconsciously give other people permission to do the same. As we are liberated from our own fear, our presence automatically liberates others."
— Marianne Williamson

When I think about balancing new school technology with ol' school simplicity, the situation that comes to mind is one that includes my two best girlfriends, Chelsea and Claire, and me communicating through Marco Polo. Chelsea and I live in New Jersey, while Claire lives in South Carolina, so it's a perfect channel for us to stay connected while we're going about our busy lives. That is, until something crucial is happening, and the "video walkie-talkie" communication is not enough. One of us then sends a text message saying, "Can you hop on a phone call or Facetime?" We all know that means we need a real-time, verbal conversation.

While the three of us use this technological application that gives us the freedom to stay in contact each day as we navigate the school of life together, we're clear it's not a replacement for direct verbal or in-person communication. A few years back, when Claire told us she was coming to town for a concert, we didn't say, "Oh, cool. We'll Marco Polo you while you're here." We immediately figured out when and how we'd meet up because nothing solidifies the bond of friendship more than physically being in each other's presence. In the meantime, when we cannot talk in person, and there isn't something pressing for us to discuss in the moment, we have this awesome technological outlet to keep us virtually together.

As you begin to implement the practices in this book, remember:

When you balance new school technology with ol' school simplicity, you become unstoppable.

Technology will begin to improve your communication rather than inhibit it, which will give rise to solid personal and professional relationships.

Now, let's pause for a second because you, my friend, have made it to the final chapter, which means you are a *rock star*. I'm not kidding. This shows you are one of the rare people who do not just talk the talk, but walk the walk, and I am so proud of you! So, before we continue, I would like you to finish reading this sentence, put the book down, and get up and dance around for a minute in celebration of your rock star status.

Okay, now go!

When life gives us something to celebrate, we are meant to sit in those moments and soak them up for all they're worth.

I hope you did not cheat yourself out of the endorphins that run through your body when you dance around in celebration because you deserve that. Praising yourself for any achievement or effort made toward your betterment is a habit I would love for you to adopt. Joseph McClendon III likes to say that, "Repetition is the mother of all skill, and praise is the father of it."

I profoundly love this phrase because praising ourselves is one of the main ingredients of fulfillment, yet we often have difficulty doing it. On the other hand, we have no difficulty beating ourselves up or believing the worst about ourselves. Doesn't that stink? This always reminds me of the scene in *Pretty Woman* when Julia Roberts and Richard Gere are lying in bed, and he says to her, "I think you are a very bright, very special woman," and she responds, "The bad stuff is easier to believe." You ever notice that? We are more apt to believe all the negative crap we tell ourselves and that others tell us than we are to believe the positive. I find this stronger belief in the negative comes from a habitual pattern of perfectionism.

Perfectionism

"Because underneath that shiny veneer, perfectionism is nothing more than a deep existential angst that says, again and again, 'I am not good enough, and I will never be good enough.'"
— Elizabeth Gilbert

Perfectionism is a complex quality because, on the surface, it can seem quite positive—a quality that drives you to be your best and holds you to a higher standard above the status quo. It is a quality that motivates you to reach goals that may appear unattainable but you believe are possible. That sounds pretty tremendous, huh? Well, I can tell you firsthand that this quality does make for some incredible strides, but at a cost. So, what do you think the cost could be of holding yourself up to sometimes impossible standards and speaking to yourself in ways you would never speak to someone else? What do you think the cost is of never letting yourself off the hook until you have achieved A, B, C, and all the way up to Z?

Perfectionism makes you believe your worthiness is conditional!

Therefore, the cost of perfectionism, my friend, is astronomically high. Your worthiness is *not* conditional but rather innately unconditional—you are worthy just because you exist.

Often, the high cost of perfectionism also includes physical strain from working intensely for long periods without sleep and from eating anything you can get your hands on. The tax on top of the cost is your mental health, which is sacrificed to the constant psychological battle between your ego and reality, with ego slandering your character until you've achieved what you've decided must be achieved.

The perfectionist mindset, whether consciously or unconsciously, believes you're only worthy if you're in a constant state of achieving—and achieving the nearly *impossible* standards you set for yourself. You're only worthy if you are what you believe is the best. You're only worthy if others approve of you, and are giving you praise.

All of the turmoil from the need to achieve arises from the underlying belief of inadequacy.

Most people feel inadequate from time to time, but for perfectionists, that feeling is on steroids. With them, inadequacy is anything short of perfection, which can lead to constantly feeling "less than" because, as you know, life isn't perfect, and neither are we as human beings.

So, when perfectionists fall short of what they perceive as perfection, whether it be with themselves or in something they want to attain, feeling inadequate pressures them to keep attaining. However, they need everything to be perfect before making a move to attain, but nothing is ever perfect, so they become stuck and feel inadequate again.

Can you see how perfectionism is a vicious cycle?

***Wanting to be your best is a beautiful intention
when the journey there is one of self-love and not self-battle.***

Are you ready to be your best from a place of self-love?

Reflections Section: *Perfectionism*

- Are you now, or have you been a perfectionist? If so, in what areas?

_____

_____

_____

_____

- What is the upside of being a perfectionist?

_____

_____

_____

_____

• What has being a perfectionist cost you?

_____

_____

_____

_____

Taking Imperfect Action

"Start before you are ready. Don't prepare, begin!"
— Mel Robbins

As a woman who lived many years as a perfectionist, I deeply understand the tendency to *not* take action until you feel you are 100 percent ready and the circumstances are just right. That way of living stresses you out, frustrates you, and holds you back from taking any action at all. You use perfectionism as an excuse to procrastinate because deep down the fear of failure, or the fear of not being good enough, is so strong you'd rather not try than risk failure.

Now, as a "reformed perfectionist," I have found that the way to combat the veil of perfectionism is through *imperfect action*. This means taking action before my mind believes I'm ready or the conditions are exactly how I'd want them to be. See, the brain will always come up with reasons you should not move forward, why you're not good enough to live out your dreams, and why you're better off just sticking to what you know. The secret here is that we must be smarter than our brains and know those reasons are not real—they are fear (False Evidence Appearing Real)—and we have no time to pay attention to what's not real. We have moves to make, dreams to catch, joy to experience, and hearts to touch. So, imperfect action is the catalyst for making these things happen.

*When we take imperfect action, we prove to ourselves
that we can do things before we're ready, and
that proof gives us nuggets of confidence that build upon
one another to create an armor of self-belief.*

Boom. Then we are ready to take on the world.

When we talked about perfect practice earlier, it meant putting everything you have into that practice, from your energy to your intention to do your best. That did not mean with no mishaps or mistakes. Mistakes become the easy part to fix when your entire heart and soul are present while you're practicing. Remember, "full out" as opposed to "half-hearted" is what perfect practice means.

This same concept is also embodied in imperfect action. Imperfect action is about jumping in wholly and entirely, even though we may not have everything figured out, and we may make mistakes along the way.

*We can perfectly practice taking imperfect action
as an antidote to perfectionism.*

(Say that five times fast.)

When you hear those words *imperfect action*, do you feel the pressure leave your body? For a reformed perfectionist like myself, going from the belief that "I have to be perfect before I take action," to "I can take imperfect action" gives me such a sense of relief.

I now feel at ease when I attempt something new, as opposed to fearing I won't be good at it. I have permission to throw caution to the wind in my endeavors and enjoy the ride. When you begin to perfectly practice imperfect action, you are able to accomplish more, but also revel in those accomplishments as you are taking the action.

Reflections Section: *Taking Imperfect Action*

- What does *imperfect action* mean to you?

_____

_____

- Are you ready to take *imperfect action*?

_____

_____

Celebrating Yourself

"My whole teaching is this;
accept yourself, love yourself, and celebrate yourself."
— Osho

We need to revisit celebrating yourself because it can keep self-judgment from creeping back in and trying to stop you on your journey. How often do you celebrate yourself? Does it take you doing something monumental? When you celebrate, does the celebration consist only of five minutes of joy or less before you move on to the next thing you have to get done? If you realize that self-celebration has not been a major priority for you, then I'd like for you first to shout out "YES!" for realizing that, and then decide *now* that celebrating yourself will become not just a priority but a *must*.

As we talked about earlier, anything we express gratitude for shows up more in our lives. When we celebrate ourselves, we are essentially expressing gratitude to ourselves for something that we've done, or for simply being who we are. This makes our mind think, *Oh, I got rewarded for that; let's look for more ways to get rewarded!* Then the mind tunes into every little positive thing we do and the positive qualities we have, and that practice becomes a habit, and that habit becomes a pattern of self-celebration. Self-celebration puts us in a state of looking forward to trying new things, and being okay with making mistakes because we know we will celebrate those mistakes for learning from them.

Now, I don't care about what you do or what you notice about yourself, but what I do care about is that you celebrate yourself for it.

If you remember to move the recycling bin to the front of the house on recycling day when you usually forget, I want you to celebrate. If you organized your kitchen drawers, celebrate. If you took a deep breath before reacting to a person who constantly pushes your buttons, celebrate. If you made someone smile by genuinely complimenting them, celebrate. If you cooked a beautiful meal that made your family happy, celebrate. If you caught yourself being rude to your spouse, and gave them a heart-felt apology, celebrate. If you recognize that you're going through a tough time spiritually and emotionally, but you're doing your best, celebrate. When you decide you will no longer tolerate being disrespected by someone and tell them so, celebrate!

How good do you think doing this will feel? *Amazing* is correct. When you start finding more things to celebrate about yourself, you will feel a beautiful energy of love gently washing over you. That beautiful energy is your soul saying, "Thank you for honoring me."

I'm going to tell you a little secret. Whenever I sit down on the floor to stretch after a workout, I give each leg a little kiss and say, "I love you." In that moment, when I'm grateful for all that my legs do for me, I immediately feel that energy of love wash over me.

Those little kisses are my way of celebrating myself, and as silly as that may sound, because I take a second to honor myself for the workout, I look forward to the next workout. When I write for an hour a day and then become my own cheerleader when that hour is up, you better believe I can't wait to sit down at my desk to write the following day.

So, my friend, let's take this celebrating yourself idea to heart and find every possible way to put it into imperfect action. If you feel silly jumping up and down and screaming "I'm amazing" in your kitchen for nailing the French toast, then go about it differently. Still jump around, but instead of screaming aloud, whisper a phrase like, "There is nothing I can't do!" The power in our words is real, but the power in our words while we move our bodies is immeasurable.

As you answer the questions below, put a smile on your face as you write down things that happened in the past two days that you could celebrate. Then write down how you will celebrate and what empowering phrases, which I call, "I Claim Statements," you will use. "I Claim Statements" are phrases that declare you already have that which you desire. For example, "I claim perfect health," "I claim true confidence," "I claim I'm a master communicator."

Remember, it doesn't matter how big or small your accomplishments are because the small things *are* the big things.

Reflections Section: *Celebrating Yourself*

- List some things you did in the past two days you can celebrate.

_____

_____

_____

_____

_____

- How will you celebrate? (Examples: Will you dance around, call a friend, put on your favorite outfit?)

_____

_____

_____

_____

- What are some "I Claim Statements" you can use to celebrate yourself? (Examples: "I claim I'm unstoppable," "I claim I'm fearless," "I claim I'm a master communicator.")

_____

_____

_____

_____

_____

ANSWERING THE
FINAL QUESTION

*"And the day came when the risk to remain tight in a bud was
more painful than the risk it took to blossom."*
— Anaïs Nin

After everything you've learned during our time together, I do have one last question:

Who do you want to be?

We are often asked *what do you want* or *what do you want to be*, but we are not often asked *who do you want to be?*

I believe when you answer this question, all of the other answers to all of the other questions fall into place. The person you want to be signifies what you will attract into your life, who you will surround yourself with, and the things you will and won't partake in based on how those things line up with your morals. Do you want to be a person who reads a book like this, and enjoys it for the moment, but never implements what you learned? On the flip side, do you want to be a follow-through person who reads a book like this, takes one practice each day to implement, and then documents what that implementation brought about?

I will say this: If you want to be the latter, you will be stacking win upon win and skyrocketing to the next level of your life faster than you can imagine. I pose this question to you, my friend, because I want you to see the two paths clearly so you can choose *now* and waste no more time pretending otherwise. I value you and have loved being your guide on this journey, so I want you to understand this very important principle.

If you don't, you won't.

This phrase means that if you don't make a move to do the things you say you *want* to do *now*, then you won't. The best time to start is when what you want is fresh in your mind and heart. One small step starts the train in motion. Otherwise, by waiting to begin, you invite the intricacies of life to side-track you, increasing the chance that you won't begin.

If you don't, you won't.

The principle is as simple as the sentence. So, I ask you once again, who do you want to be? If you want to be the person I believe you *want* to be—an *imperfect action taker* toward living your best life, then start now. If you want to be the person who has the confidence to speak up for what you feel and desire, and you want to build powerful relationships by becoming a master communicator, then start *now*. You have all the tools you need in your toolbox.

In closing, I want to remind you of something that is imperative. When you're using social media, please remember that just like Instagram has "stories," all of the posts and photos you see are just that—stories. They are snippets of people's lives that they give us permission to see. It's key to understand there are many more parts of their lives we do not see. No one is taking snapshots of arguments or when they don't like the way their bodies look or when they are in their rooms by themselves crying tears from deep emotional wounds. Think about this the next time you start to compare yourself to someone in any way, because, as Iyanla Vanzant stated so beautifully, "Comparison is an act of violence against the self."

Instead of comparing yourself to someone else's perceived reality, go out into the world and live!

I mean really live. Keep your head up and be present in nature. Meet a friend who lights up your spirit for coffee and laugh your butt off. Take a road trip, be spontaneous, give love, learn something new, forget about posting your life and *live it*! There is a time and place for digital technology, but always remember there must also be a time and place for simplicity and coming back home to ourselves. Then, when we pick up our phone or computer, we are coming from a place of balance, allowing us to have the best of both worlds: The world of *"New School Technology"* with *"Ol' School Simplicity!"*

Here's to being master communicators and having the best that authentic communication has to offer.

With Love and Complete Gratitude,

Renée Marino

"Yesterday I was clever, so I wanted to change the world.
Today I am wise, so I am changing myself."
— Rumi

Reflections Section: *Answering the Final Question*

- Who do you want to be?

_____

_____

_____

_____

_____

REFERENCES

Introduction

1. Gazzaley, Adam and Larry D. Rosen. *The Distracted Mind: Ancient Brains in a High-Tech World.* Cambridge, MA: MIT Press, 2016.

Chapter One

1. Hart, C. H., Newell, L. D., & Olsen, S. F. (2003). "Parenting Skills and Social-Communicative Competence in Childhood." In J. O. Greene & B. R. Burleson (eds.). *Handbook of Communication and Social Interaction Skills.* Lawrence Erlbaum Associates Publishers. p. 753–797.

Chapter Two

1. Cartwright, Mark. "Yin and Yang." *Ancient History Encyclopedia.* Last modified May 16, 2018. https://www.ancient.eu/Yin_and_Yang/.
2. Gazzaley, Adam and Larry D. Rosen. *The Distracted Mind: Ancient Brains in a High-Tech World.* Cambridge, MA: MIT Press, 2016.
3. Benbunan-Fich, Raquel. (2012). "The Ethics and Etiquette of Multitasking in the Workplace." *Technology and Society Magazine.* 31 (2012): 15-19.

4. Turkle, Sherry. *Alone Together: Why We Expect More From Technology and Less from Each Other.* New York: Basic Books, 2011. p. 161.

5. https://www.business.com/articles/video-content-marketing-for-business/.

6. https://www.actionagainsthunger.org/world-hunger-facts-statistics #:~:text=Around%20the%20world%2C%20more%20than,million %20people%20still%20go%20hungry.

7. Ellanti, P. et al. "The Use of WhatsApp Smartphone Messaging Improves Communication Efficiency Within an Orthopaedic Surgery Team." *Cureus.* 2017. 9(2):e1040. Published 2017 Feb 18. doi:10.7759/cureus.1040.

Chapter Three

1. Turkle, Sherry. *Alone Together: Why We Expect More From Technology and Less From Each Other.* New York: Basic Books, 2011. p. 167.

2. Ibid.

3. Pratt, Madara and Sarma Cakula. "The Impact of Using Technology-Based Communication on Quality of Work Relationships." *Baltic J. Modern Computing.* 8.1 (2020): 143-153. https://doi.org/10.22364/bjmc.2020.8.1.07.

4. Ibid.

Chapter Four

1. Kramarae, Cheris. "Technology and Women's Voices." 1988. Routledge, Chapman and Hall, New York. Reviewed in *Bulletin of Science, Technology & Society.* 10.3 (June 1990): 138. https://doi.org/10.1177/027046769001000318.

2. Gazzaley, Adam and Larry D. Rosen. *The Distracted Mind: Ancient Brains in a High-Tech World.* Cambridge, MA: MIT Press, 2016.

3. Taylor, Jim. "How Technology Is Changing the Way Children Think and Focus." *Psychology Today.* December 4, 2012. https://www.psychologytoday.com/us/blog/the-power-prime/201212/how-technology-is-changing-the-way-children-think-and-focus.

4. Kwik, Jim. *Limitless: Upgrade Your Brain, Learn Anything Faster, and Unlock Your Exceptional Life.* Carlsbad, CA: Hay House, 2020.

5. Ophir, Eyal et al. "Cognitive Control in Media Multitaskers." *Proceedings of the National Academy of Sciences of the United States of America.* 106.37 (2009): 15583-7. doi:10.1073/pnas.0903620106.

6. Steves, Rick. *Rick Steves Italy 2018.* New York: Avalon Travel Publishing, 2017. p. 6.

7. Misra, Shalini et al. "The iPhone Effect: The Quality of In-Person Social Interactions in the Presence of Mobile Devices." *Environment and Behavior.* 48 (2014). 10.1177/0013916514539755.

Chapter Five

1. Kuss, D. J., Griffiths, M. D. "Social Networking Sites and Addiction: Ten Lessons Learned." *Int J Environ Res Public Health.* 14.3(2017): 311. doi:10.3390/ijerph14030311.

2. NPR. "Digital Overload: Your Brain on Gadgets." Last modified August 24, 2010. www.npr.org/templates/story/story.php?storyId=129384107.

ABOUT THE AUTHOR

Renée Marino is a professional communication coach named by Yahoo Finance as one of the "Top 10 Communication Coaches to Follow in 2021!" She was the co-host of Tony Robbins and Dean Graziosi's first-ever virtual "World Summit" and has spoken, performed, and been interviewed on thousands of live and virtual stages, including Dean Graziosi's podcast *The Dean Graziosi Show*. Renée helps people create genuine connections in their life and business by balancing new school technology with ol' school simplicity. She also uses her well-rounded experience of communicating through various mediums to train companies, organizations, schools, and universities in strengthening their communication skills.

Renée can be seen as the female lead, Mary Delgado, in the film *Jersey Boys*, directed by Clint Eastwood. She has been featured in People.com's

"Ones to Watch," *Variety*, and *The Huffington Post*, which stated: "The Broadway star—who is basically Tina Fey's celebrity doppelganger—is a scene-stealer, spouting swears and put-downs with aplomb. 'Jersey Boys' pops whenever she's onscreen." Renée wrote and performed her solo show, *I Am Me, Because of Three*, to sold-out venues in NYC and LA and received rave reviews.

Her Broadway credits include *Pretty Woman: The Musical* (dance captain/assistant to the choreographer/ensemble), *West Side Story* (Rosalia), *Jersey Boys* (Mary Delgado), *Chaplin*, and *Wonderland* (ensemble). She has toured North America with *Cats*, *Disney's High School Musical*, and *Jersey Boys*. Her television credits include Regina on Fox's *Weird Loners* and *The Marvelous Mrs. Maisel*.

As a coach, keynote speaker, and longtime performer, Renée Marino has inspired people worldwide with her energy, relatability, and authentic spirit.

For more information, visit:

ReneeMarino.com
Instagram: @IAmReneeMarino
Facebook: @CoachReneeMarino
Twitter: @ReneeMarino
LinkedIn: @RenéeMarino
YouTube: ReneeMarino

CONTINUE THE JOURNEY
WITH RENÉE

R enée Marino teaches a live workshop course called "Connecting on Camera" that helps individuals get past what is holding them back when it comes to being on video. Through her structured and simple process, individuals learn to bring their real and most confident selves to the camera, whether for virtual meetings, video calls, live videos, or standard ones.

Renée also coaches people one-on-one whether to connect on camera or strengthen communication within their relationships by using the tools from *Becoming a Master Communicator*.

Renée trains companies, organizations, schools, and universities on how to:

- Enhance communication among their teams and with their clients both physically and virtually.
- Run effective virtual meetings.
- Genuinely connect in physical and virtual interviews.
- Improve communication between teachers and students in physical and virtual educational settings.
- Create positive and productive work atmospheres.

Renée is also a well-versed keynote speaker. She speaks on numerous topics, including:

- How to Become a Master Communicator
- The Power of Communication with Self
- Great Leadership Begins with Great Communication
- Taking Imperfect Action
- Communication is the Key to Relationship Building

For more information about how Renée can help you or your organization, visit:

ReneeMarino.com
Instagram: @IAmReneeMarino
Facebook: @CoachReneeMarino
Twitter: @ReneeMarino
LinkedIn: @RenéeMarino

A free ebook edition is available with the purchase of this book.

To claim your free ebook edition:

1. Visit MorganJamesBOGO.com
2. Sign your name CLEARLY in the space
3. Complete the form and submit a photo of the entire copyright page
4. You or your friend can download the ebook to your preferred device

Morgan James
BOGO™

A **FREE** ebook edition is available for you or a friend with the purchase of this print book.

CLEARLY SIGN YOUR NAME ABOVE

Instructions to claim your free ebook edition:
1. Visit MorganJamesBOGO.com
2. Sign your name CLEARLY in the space above
3. Complete the form and submit a photo of this entire page
4. You or your friend can download the ebook to your preferred device

Print & Digital Together Forever.

Snap a photo

Free ebook

Read anywhere

Printed in the USA
CPSIA information can be obtained
at www.ICGtesting.com
JSHW022321140824
68134JS00019B/1224

9 781631 956003